WN
ARIES
RENEWALS 691-4574
DATE DUE

POLICE ARREST AND SEARCH

Nemesis of Policework

POLICE ARREST AND SEARCH

By

HERBERT PHILLIP VALLOW

Lewistown, Pennsylvania

CHARLES C THOMAS • PUBLISHER

Springfield · Illinois · U.S.A.

Published and Distributed Throughout the World by
CHARLES C THOMAS · PUBLISHER
BANNERSTONE HOUSE
301-327 East Lawrence Avenue, Springfield, Illinois, U.S.A.

This book is protected by copyright. No
part of it may be reproduced in any manner
without written permission from the publisher.

© *1962, by* CHARLES C THOMAS · PUBLISHER
Library of Congress Catalog Card Number: 62-17616

*With THOMAS BOOKS careful attention is given to all details of
manufacturing and design. It is the Publisher's desire to present books
that are satisfactory as to their physical qualities and artistic possibilities
and appropriate for their particular use. THOMAS BOOKS will be true
to those laws of quality that assure a good name and good will.*

LIBRARY
University of Texas
At San Antonio

Printed in the United States of America.

DEDICATION

*To the countless ranks of brave men who
gave their lives that others might live in a
society of law and order—and among them
my friends—this book is dedicated in the
hope that—if the file—constantly moving
to join them—is interrupted—even by one
—their rest may be more peaceful*

PREFACE

The author gratefully acknowledges indebtedness to the United States Army, under whose auspices he was able to develop a number of techniques contained in this text to the extent that they were adopted as army-wide doctrine in June 1952.

In its present form, it is in no way intended as containing any indorsements but, instead, all techniques presented are solely the opinions of the author.

ACKNOWLEDGMENTS

The author acknowledges sincere gratitude to Lee G. Lyter, Chief of Police of the Lewistown, Pennsylvania, Police Department, for his cooperation in providing the services of Sergeant Orrie A. Snook and Patrolman John R. Yocum III, for the photographs contained in this text; to The Honorable Paul S. Lehman, President Judge of the 58th Judicial District of the Commonwealth of Pennsylvania, sincere appreciation for indicating the direction that research should take in developing the legal principles cited in Chapter 3. Finally, it is with heartfelt thanks that indebtedness is acknowledged to Brigadier General Edward F. Penaat, United States Army, whose catalytic efforts engendered the original formulation of these thoughts. The drawings are by Anita M. Leo. The photographs are by W. Shields.

H.P.V.

CONTENTS

POLICE ARREST AND SEARCH

CHAPTER 1

INTRODUCTION

WHY THE TEXT?

The stench of death has an all-prevailing intoxication. Its anxiety-producing effects seep into the mind, quelling the ability to reason, reducing functional reaction to a pre-conditioned, primitive state totally devoid of recourse to logic, intellect, and application of common sense usually present in the contemporary product of evolution—the human mind.

In hindsight we are amazed at the carelessness of our past actions, unable to explain the absence of our usual efficiency. We believe that we should have been more capable and, yet, without an understanding of the devastating affects of our tensions, we are unable to provide a comprehensible explanation.

This principle, with little popular acknowledgment, is the greatest contributor to the death of innumerable, otherwise competent, policemen. Its importance can better be realized by an awareness that statistically, if a policeman is going to be killed, it will almost of a certainty be during his attempt to make an arrest.

There is another type of duty which contributes considerably to the high mortality rate of police work: death or maiming from an automobile accident while fulfilling the requirements of traffic control, but this source is comparatively insignificant in degree to the number of policemen constantly killed while making the arrest.

Further study reveals that fatalities of this sort will occur as the definite result of some seemingly insignificant, thoughtless mistake or mishap. In reexamining the chain of circumstance, it is almost always found that it was not an unusual danger or brilliance on the part of the individual being arrested that was the causative factor, but, instead, an act of negligence on the part of the policeman so gross that it almost appears improbable.

In fact, because these mistakes are so basic, it is difficult to develop a sufficient appreciation of their seriousness. This burden, together with the problems it creates, was a factor of which I became particularly aware only after years of teaching these techniques in the classroom.

The military has long been aware of this principle as applicable in other areas. Resolution is provided by repetitious drill sufficient to the extent that the recruit, by the time he is exposed to the tensions of combat, has developed habit formations incorporating procedures that save his life and create automatic reactions even though the terrors of combat can, at times, almost completely nullify his intellectual facilities.

The subject matter I was required to present concerned basic principles which appeared so simple, that at times they were boring. The students, reacting accordingly, would frequently become apathetic, believing that because of their simplicity the elements were so unimportant as to require little or no atttention.

Prior to assuming the duties of a teacher I had experienced the deaths of too many subordinates because of mistakes involving these same simple elements and, as a result, this student reaction caused a great deal of consternation. In an effort to enliven the subject I attempted to interject humor and countless hundreds heard of the questionable antics of "Shma-ha Joe" and "Gazonski Pete," who were my own creative personifications of all the idiocies encountered in policework.

Unfortunately, however, death is no laughing matter, and this could not provide the necessary rectification. The student, in the classroom, just couldn't grasp the importance of studying how to hold a gun or use his voice. The reason for this is quite simple. In the non-stressful atmosphere of the classroom the subject matter seemed too unimportant, and each student reasoned that he was capable enough to apply common sense, therefore no special skills were needed. After all, it was just common sense. It therefore became of considerable importance to create an awareness that the tensions of an arrest in a dangerous situation could easily wipe out the student's ability to apply common sense.

And so, after months of frustration, a practical exercise in application of these mechanics under tension was engendered, later commonly referred to as "The Horror Chamber."

Mr. Erle Stanley Gardner, a very kind gentleman, subsequently wrote an article describing its unusual approach which appeared in *The Saturday Evening Post.* Additional "glamour" was derived when Universal-International made a movie of its actual operation.

However, the intent and purpose of the exercise was deadly serious. I had set out to mentally take the student out of the peaceful atmosphere of the classroom and, by creating enough tension, produce a sufficiently stressful situation to bear some semblance to a real-life arrest under dangerous circumstances. My methods may have been highly irregular, for I utilized every device available, from automobile sirens to shots in dark closets, so that by the time the student appeared on stage, in front of floodlights and the cynical observation of his classmates, he was a mass of tensions.

The exercise in itself was simple. Two students were required to enter into a murder scene and arrest the culprits. If application of the principles previously taught in the classroom was accomplished, they achieved a perfect score; but, if they failed to apply these techniques, for the purpose of the problem, they were considered to have been killed.

No particularly complex problems were required to be resolved, yet during the following years several thousand students, many of them active policemen, sheriffs, constables, officers and enlisted men of the American Army, Navy, Coast Guard, and Marine Corps, Canadian Army, English Army and other foreign armies, gloriously marched to their simulated deaths, each the victim of a ridiculously careless mistake, the result of tensions I had been able to evoke.

Ironically, these tensions were not as great as those prevalent in actual circumstances when the arresting policeman is aware that a mistake will result in his death.

Out of a class of a hundred students it was a statistical certainty that ninety-eight would not successfully complete the exercise.

In classroom presentation, the simple procedure of depressing the safety lever on an automatic pistol appeared to the student so basic that he could barely refrain from yawning. On the stage it was a different matter as evidenced by the hundreds, wildly squeezing the trigger, in panic because the gun would not fire. This, the result of their having forgotten to depress the safety lever.

When the axiom of always searching an individual who was arrested was presented in the classroom, the student, bored, sought relief by occupying his mind with more important factors. While on stage I would witness these same students manifesting the opposite reaction while attempting to herd prisoners with guns prominently protruding from their belts and knives clearly evident in their shirt cuffs.

The student reaction as a whole became ludicrous; however, my own appreciation of its humor was strongly dampened as unfortunately the memories were too vivid of my own men and former friends who had more realistically paid for these same mistakes—with their lives.

CURRENT IMPORTANCE

Today, all too frequently a coldly objective article appears in the paper or a commentator, with seemingly unconcerned tones, cites the most recent death of a peace officer who gave his life "in the line of duty." In each instance I strongly suspect from the same irrelevant causes.

It is not the purpose of this text to provide some fabulous panacea that will resolve this entire problem, or a magic formula that, once learned, will safeguard the lives of the readers. There is no infallible scheme with a money-back guarantee. No procedure, no principle, no technique can act as a substitute for the necessary training and alertness of the policeman. Even the principles as presented in this text, as basic as they seem, are valueless unless the student is constantly trained and retrained in their proper application until he has developed a habit formation that will automatically occur no matter what his mental state.

Make no mistake, the experienced policeman is just as vulnerable as the rookie, at times even more so. The rookie is not lulled into a false sense of security by over-confidence. He is even more aware of the close proximity of death, a factor that, by over-familiarity, causes the old-timer a narcotic reaction, lulling him into a routine that too easily results in a fatal mistake.

Most vividly do I recall an experience that involved a federal narcotics agent (to my way of thinking the most competent policemen in the world), who had been sent to the school following an arrest which had resulted in the death of his partner, and himself being critically wounded in the stomach. After proceeding through the exercise, there was no humor in his voice while remarking that, had he and his companion previously experienced this training, his partner would still be alive and he would not have suffered the agonies of his unnecessary wound.

LOCAL MODIFICATION

Techniques as described here are formulated for the police team approach. This is so because, to my way of thinking, it is the ideal approach. I am well aware, however, that in many police organizations they are not afforded this facility. Slight modification can still retain the value of these principles where it is necessary for the peace officer to act independently.

As it is impossible to totally separate legal requirements from the mechanics involved, some reference is made to those legal procedures that are most frequently encountered in any locale. The new student, however, is strongly advised to thoroughly acquaint himself with the applicable laws of his own geographical jurisdiction and, where necessary, accordingly modify his own policies.

All in all, the entire text is not presented in the vein that it is the only or perfect solution. Instead, as simple and basic as its scope is intended, if sufficient thought (even if controversial) is forthcoming, and, with the necessary training, applied, the resulting lives that are saved will be well worth the author's effort.

EXAMINATION

1. Considering the entire police field, what duty requirement is the most dangerous?
2. What are the two most important elements necessary for a safe arrest?
3. Is the experienced peace officer less vulnerable to injury than the rookie in an arrest? Why?

4. What signs should the policeman look for to warn him that an arrest may become dangerous?
5. What facial features should the policeman look for to warn him that the suspect is a potential killer?
6. In arresting a dangerous individual, if a mistake is made, what recourse does the policeman have?

CHAPTER 2

THE CONTROL OF AN ARREST

ATTITUDE

Common sense dictates that, from the very beginning, the peace officer must gain control of the situation and, throughout the arrest, retain this control.

How this is accomplished, because of the many nuances involved, is difficult to describe, and is as equally difficult to grasp and put into effect.

The principles involved may bear strong resemblances to those encountered in certain dynamic courses found in the business world, or in those schools prescribing "positive thinking." But make no mistake about their importance. They concern a form of communication that does not necessarily involve speaking, but rather through manner, attitude, appearance and actions, impresses the suspect with our true frame of mind. Usually these communications have as their source our mental image of ourselves.

Here the experienced policeman is at a distinct advantage. He has been "through the acid test," so to speak. He is accustomed to being obeyed and he communicates this attitude by his whole approach.

The rookie, on the other hand, is uncertain and commits little irregularities. Whether these are hesitancies or over-emphasis they are tell-tale signs, surprisingly easily communicated and causing untold difficulties.

To correct this our first and foremost consideration must be —attitude. Effective display of other elements necessary to control an arrest are dependent to a great degree upon this.

Proper attitude is initially achieved by constantly remembering that the primary function of any peace officer is to preserve law and order. The peace officer must never forget that in making an arrest he is performing an official act. During the arrest he is the symbol of law and order. He must be impartial and impersonal. This attitude must be reflected in his language and actions at all times, usually by adopting firm and courteous methods.

Police work is not to be used as a substitute for "growing up." When in doubt, it is much safer to find some other means of proving one's manhood. Contact with the suspect should never be reduced to a level of personal emotional encounter. Instead, the policeman must develop and at all times maintain a professional attitude clearly indicating objective thinking.

In plainer English, the attitude should be: "I have a job to do which I definitely will successfully complete." and not, "This is me against you, and I have a personal grudge against you."

If this principle is not adherred to, and the policeman reflects in his voice, stance, or demeanor an "emotional conflict" or "I'm a tougher guy than you," attitude, he will remove the act from its necessary professional realm and usually provoke an otherwise tractable suspect into unnecessary resistance. This will occur especially if the suspect is as immature and has equal doubts of masculinity. The entire situation will usually be reduced to an emotional conflict of "who is the bigger man."

There are two general methods of securing an individual's compliance with an order.

The first, to treat the suspect with unwarranted belligerence in the hope of frightening him into obedience. This, of course, has many serious drawbacks. It reflects the officer's unconscious fear of inadequacy, one which the suspect, especially if he is versed in psychology, is quick to recognize and take advantage of.

It can also have the opposite effect in the case of the naive suspect who becomes overimpressed and actually does get frightened to the extent that he believes his welfare is in jeopardy. To the uninitiated the loss of liberty can become a panic-provoking act. As a matter of course he frequently resorts to extreme measures in an effort to protect himself.

One cardinal rule the arresting peace officer must never forget is that, barring none, *the most dangerous individual to deal with is a panic-stricken one.*

In the opinion of the author, from the perspective of self-preservation, the arrest of a professional killer suspected of murder is less dangerous than the arrest of a frightened juvenile with a zip-gun. The professional killer believes that there is always some "angle" he can later rely upon, whereas the frightened juvenile, in his panic-stricken state, is more prone to act on impulse, resorting to extreme measures in blind, terror-stricken disregard of consequences.

Attempting to interject fear in the mind of a suspect can be the spark that results in reactions totally out of proportion.

Instead, the second and better method of securing the suspect's compliance is—by example. This can be accomplished by conveying the attitude of firmness, mature judgment, utilizing tact and self-control at all times. This, of course, is the much more proficient and prescribed method.

From previous experience it has been noted that certain patrols (consisting of either one or two man teams) developed an exceptionally high record of incidents involving "difficult and complicated arrests," whereas, in comparison, other teams seemed to consistently make "smooth and uncomplicated arrests." The former, although initially starting out with a simple arrest, usually would end up in difficulties.

Study revealed that in almost every case the belligerent attitude of the individual patrolman or team was the basic causative factor.

A simple but surprisingly important rule is to treat the suspect as the peace officer himself would like to be treated. In the majority of instances a subject who is treated fairly, and whose self-respect is not threatened, normally offers little resistance.

A little courtesy goes a long way in securing the suspect's compliance. Certainly nothing imparts as professional an air as a firm and courteous policeman. It almost always imparts the communication that he is sufficiently confident that it is not necessary to rely on any "act of toughness" to achieve successful results.

Conversely, the rookie frequently has the tendency to assume the role of a "good guy."

All of us like to be liked; this is human nature. In dealing with other humans we frequently if unnecessarily attempt to secure their "good graces."

In contradiction to this, the arresting officer must never forget that, no matter by what name it is called, *an arrest is an act that deprives an individual of his liberty.* This is supported from a professional perspective (and definitely a safety perspective) by the cardinal rule that *once an individual is arrested no favors or special requests are to be granted.*

In the movies or on television the "gruff old cop with the heart of gold" depicts entreating melodrama. In reality the arresting peace officer has only to violate or forget this rule one time and the resulting cost can be his life.

Too many occurrences of this violation resulted in the death of otherwise capable policemen who have "just this one time given the guy a break." No departure from this policy is ever warranted. Alleviating special concerns or problems of the suspect can always be accomplished in the safety of the station house or police lockup in the due course of time.

The peace officer, unless he has a knack of reading minds, can never tell what threat the arrest represents to the suspect. Although the arrest may appear to be based only upon a charge, simple in nature, the suspect may have knowledge of a much more serious, previous offense. This in turn giving rise to the fear that the "simple" arrest will lead to its extremely more severe conse quences.

The rookie will also, during his initial experiences, frequently have many doubts concerning his competency and whether the suspect will obey his commands. Time usually will alleviate this doubt, however, the wrong arrest during the initial stages does not afford the rookie this necessary time.

Even the experienced policeman will occasionally come upon a scene that is bewildering in its confusion. Once he allows doubt to creep into his attitude at the initiation of the arrest, it is too late to attempt to develop an appearance of competence in further sequences of the action.

Regardless of the case, whether the experience is novel, or extremely confusing, or the arresting peace officer is assailed by many personal doubts, if he betrays these doubts, the suspect (especially the habitual offender) is quick to recognize this and take advantage of it.

When first arriving at the scene of an incident there is usually a certain amount of confusion in the mind of any peace officer concerning what has previously taken place and what is the best future course of action to take. He must not allow this uncertainty to show but, instead, must start from the beginning manifesting a firm, confident manner.

This does not mean "bluffing." It means that the peace officer attempts to divest emotional colorings from his actions as much as possible. *During the arrest the competent peace officer never makes a threat unless he has the means of fulfilling it and actually intends to carry it out.*

Developing this professional appearance of confidence is easier said than done. Possibly, considering some elements of attitude will ease this accomplishment.

The rookie should not become indecisive because he is afraid of making a mistake. It is much more sensible to take a chance, make a mistake, and even look ridiculous, than to die proudly. Most experience is gained by making mistakes and profiting from them. Where he fails to understand this and becomes indecisive, the rookie will, as a matter of course, allow this doubt in his attitude to be reflected in his manner.

The approach to the arrest scene should be made with an open mind, but as quickly as possible the peace officer should decide on his proper course of action and, even if some doubts remain, he should firmly proceed along this course of action.

In the following paragraphs the factors presented, as necessary to gain control at the scene of the arrest, are "mirrors," so to speak, that reflect the attitude of the peace officer. If the arresting officer has been able to secure a competent and professional attitude, the use of: the voice, demeanor, and force will auto-

matically, satisfactorily adjust accordingly. All of these are out-
ward indications, dependent, to a large degree, to what goes on
in the mind of the arresting policeman.

PROPER USE OF THE VOICE

In talking, giving commands, or conveying explanations,
much more is expressed to the suspect than the words used. No
other action on the part of the peace officer can communicate
fear, doubt, or lack of self-confidence as quickly as the improper
use of the voice. Its importance cannot be over-emphasized.

Unfortunately too many officers interpret the proper use of
the voice as meaning that they must talk "tough" or loud. However, an increase of volume, rate of delivery, or resort to profane
or obscene language usually conveys the *opposite* effect. A man
who is really self-confident wastes little effort in trying to impress.
He has no doubts about his competency and is not overly concerned about proving it. Psychologists point out that the loud
"tough guy" attitude almost always indicates deep-rooted self-
doubts.

Even without the study of this science, common knowledge
gained by dealing with animals, such as a dog or a horse soon
imparts the conclusion that, if an order is given where doubt is
expressed in the tone, the animal immediately senses the doubt
and will not obey no matter how loudly it is repeated. Human
beings unconsciously react in the same way.

This is a particularly prevalent hurdle confronting the novice
when he initially engages in police work. Its resolution can best
be facilitated by "positive thinking." During this stage, when any
command is given, the rookie must actively formulate in his own
mind the conception that the order is going to be carried out and
his tone must accordingly reflect this.

The distinction is somewhat similar to the difference between
giving an order and asking a question. Where necessary, the tone
should not imply that the suspect is being *asked* to raise his hands.
The tone derived from the proper "positive thinking" indicates
that there is no doubt about it. This attitude provides a tone of

total confidence that the suspect is fully expected to raise his hands.

This particular facet is one of the most valuable keys in securing a successful, uncomplicated arrest. In general, a properly trained peace officer can accomplish more by the proper use of his voice than an incompetent one can accomplish by the use of his gun and club even though his vocabulary is liberally embellished with profanity or obscenity. Certainly, if for no other reason, recourse to this type of language reflects discreditably upon the officer's effort towards fulfilling his primary mission, that of being society's symbol of law and order.

Finally, a competent police officer rarely raises his voice except to make himself heard, never because emotion has "gotten the better of him." If, in reality, a peace officer lets emotion get the better of him, he becomes as effective as a boxer in the ring swinging blindly and wildly. Further, there is nothing to be gained by putting on an act of explosive anger where, in reality, this has not occurred. Conversely, the major effort should be directed towards producing a calming effect.

In accordance a particularly important axiom always adhered to is: *a quiet tone has an over-all calming effect.*

DEMEANOR

By his movements the peace officer can successfully support or adversely affect the same principles previously described. His stance, rate of movement, or decisiveness in his actions can communicate either competence or doubt.

First and foremost, the proper wearing of the uniform here becomes important, not because neatness reflects "spit and polish" but, instead, because its absence can too easily denote belligerence.

In the figure titled, "Incorrect, Belligerent Stance," the thought, "OK, tough guy, let's fight!" is all too clearly conveyed and, in the majority of instances, this reaction will soon be forthcoming.

It, too, implies an attitude on the part of the peace officer that the unsophisticated suspect interprets as a threat to his own welfare. He can too easily be led to believe that he cannot trust the arresting

NOT RECOMMENDED
Fig. 1.   Demeanor: Incorrect, Belligerent Stance

officers because he might suffer a severe beating. All too frequently he will react accordingly.

At the opposite extreme, the demeanor as shown in the figure titled, "Incorrect, Hysterical Stance," can by the overwrought frenzied movements of the peace officers, convey to the suspect the idea that the arresting officers are so ridiculous as to be a "pushover." Even where, initially, no thought of resistance occurred, this type of demeanor invites trouble. Nothing will cause a habitual offender to openly revolt as quickly as the thought that he "can get away with it."

The arresting peace officer should adopt a firm but comfortable stance. He should not be stiff nor "at attention;" instead, he

NOT RECOMMENDED

Fig. 2. Demeanor: Incorrect, Hysterical Stance

should stand with feet spread slightly apart, hands at his sides, displaying an air of alertness. He should always face the subject squarely.

Movement normally should be unhurried with every attempt to avoid a frenzied, nervous appearance (as indicated in the previous figure).

As is shown in the figure titled, "Correct Stance," the intent is not to convey a "Gung-Ho" attitude but, instead, this position best denotes self-confidence and a professional demeanor implying the ability to gain control of any police situation.

RECOMMENDED
Fig. 3. Demeanor: Correct Stance

EXAMINATION

1. At what point during the arrest should the peace officer attempt to gain control?
2. Considering attitude as used in gaining control of an arrest, what advantage does the experienced peace officer have over the rookie?
3. What is meant by the danger of subjective thinking during an arrest, or reducing an arrest to an emotional conflict?
4. What special requests of exceptional nature are granted the suspect after he is arrested?
5. Explain the rule concerning the use of a threat during an arrest.

6. In the opinion of the author, what type of suspect is the most dangerous?
7. What is meant when discussing the "asking a question" voice tone?
8. What beneficial effect is accomplished by the arresting officer using a calm, quiet tone?
9. Describe the correct stance of the arresting policeman.

CHAPTER 3

BASIC LEGAL ELEMENTS

APPLICABILITY

Although the scope of this text prohibits exploration in depth of applicable laws, certain basic elements are herewith defined as are considered necessary. Without at least a basic comprehension of the legal requirements, it would be difficult, if not impossible, for the reader to understand the mechanics that are described herein for their satisfaction.

Generally speaking, these legal elements are applicable in any geographic location; however, THE READER IS CAUTIONED THAT THIS TEXT IS IN NO WAY INTENDED AS A LEGAL AUTHORITY.

Sheriffs, their deputies, constables, private investigators, and special guards can only arrive at a satisfactory understanding by study of applicable statutory or municipal legislation, and the court decisions interpreting same.

In addition, it is necessary that governmental agents (civilian or military), policemen, detectives, rangers and civil defense auxiliary policemen study further modifications as contained in applicatory organizational regulations and legislation.

It is of utmost importance that the arresting peace officer thoroughly acquaint himself concerning his legal status prior to engaging in that type of police work that can necessitate an arrest. Where this status has not been clearly spelled out, it can result in indecisiveness during the arrest, with its physical danger, and other extremely severe consequences that occur when an illegal act is committed as a result of ignorance.

STATUS IDENTIFICATION

Contained within the United States Constitution and in most state constitutions are some provisions guaranteeing every citizen the right to defend his liberty. Normally, an arrest is initiated by the peace officer indicating that he has the necessary authority to set aside this right. In some instances this police burden is satisfied only by the presentation of a warrant; in others, satisfaction is accomplished simply by verbal identification.

Where a uniformed policeman is accomplishing an arrest, wherein no warrant is required, the mere wearing of the uniform normally is considered sufficient to satisfy identification during daylight hours; however, in hours of darkness or in the case of a non-uniformed detective, constable, sheriff, special agent, etc., there usually remains the burden of clearly, verbally stating that he has police authority. Frequently it is required that this be further supported by display of a badge or credentials.

This is a particularly important requirement that must be accomplished prior to the use of any applicable force or display of weapons. If the peace officer fails to accomplish this prior to the use of necessary force, or even the display of a weapon, the suspect has legal ground for reciprocatory use of force, even to the extent of deadly force, where he believes his life is in danger.

For example, in an arrest where the plainclothes peace officer rightfully made the approach with gun in hand, but failed to initially identify himself, it is not too difficult to imagine a jury's acceptance of the suspect's legal excuse that he shot and killed the arresting peace officer in self-defense because, "He didn't know that he was a policeman, thought his life was in danger from some unknown assailant, and merely took those steps necessary to protect himself."

Therefore a cardinal routine procedure must be that *every arrest is initiated by the peace officer identifying himself.*

LEGAL PROVISIONS NECESSARY TO ACCOMPLISH THE ARREST

There are additional elements that normally must be present in every arrest in order to satisfy all of the legal requirements. Some are usually mandatory; others are just good police procedures. As has previously been cited, an arrest is legally considered the act of depriving an individual of his liberty, or the taking into custody of an individual. We have also cited that the first step is this "setting aside" of the citizen's normal right of liberty.

In addition, it is usually required that he be informed of the reason for this "setting aside." In other words, the nature of the charge against him should be declared. This should be done for several reasons. First and foremost, it is a right of the citizen and, second, it can have a considerable effect upon subsequent court-room admissibility of evidence gained during the arrest.

Normally, all verbal information forthcoming during the arrest falls into two general categories. That which is spontaneous declaration is usually regarded as information forthcoming from the suspect unsolicited by the peace officer. In other words, where the suspect makes a statement that contains evidence contrary to his own best interests without having first been questioned by the peace officer, the evidence is almost always admissible in subsequent court action.

If, however, the peace officer first asks a question and then gains the information, in some instances, for it to be admissible, he must have first informed the suspect of the nature of the charge against him. There is usually another element which, under certain circumstances, must be present for admissibility, and will be described shortly.

However, in order to complete the arrest and after presentation of the previously cited originating elements—the authoritative status of the arresting peace officer together with the nature of the charge—a final factor is usually necessarily forthcoming. This can be accomplished in one of two ways.

If, after the peace officer has presented his authoritative status, and has stated the charge with the fact that the suspect is under arrest, the suspect makes any overt movement indicating his acceptance of this status, he completes the arrest.

For example, in a routine arrest where the approaching peace officer declares, "Police, you are under arrest, charged with murder. Move over to the wall," and the suspect, in contradiction to his former movements, moves in the direction that the policeman has indicated, he thereby acknowledges his acceptance of this "taking into custody" and the arrest is usually considered complete. If, however, this movement in response is not secured, the peace officer is usually required to physically touch the suspect in order to complete the arrest.

This is frequently a mandatory requirement that must be satisfied prior to a charge of "breach of arrest" in those circumstances where the suspect subsequently escapes.

Finally, although it is not commonly advocated, the author subscribes to the proposition that the peace officer always should explain the rights of the suspect under the Fifth Amendment to the Constitution. If this is not followed, it can, under certain jurisdictions, render solicited information inadmissible in subsequent court action. For, as has previously been cited, usually two factors are necessary to satisfy the rules of evidence where such evidence was secured as the result of questioning: first, that the accused was informed of the charge being investigated; and second, that he be advised of his rights under the Fifth Amendment to the Constitution. Certainly the burden of explaining these rights under the Thirty-first Article is mandatorily required for those acting under the authority of the Military Code.

The author has experienced several incidents where valuable evidence was rendered inadmissible because the arresting officer failed to satisfy these provisions at the origination of the arrest. Even under those laws where the burden of explaining the rights under the Fifth Amendment to the Constitution is not mandatorily required, the peace officer, by providing this explanation, affords himself a considerable barrier against subsequent countercharge that he received a confession through the use of duress or threat. It becomes rather difficult for a suspect to charge that he was subjected to police brutality where it can be shown that the peace officer provided more than was required of him in an effort to protect the rights of the accused.

Conversely, the author has never experienced any particular difficulty in securing statements against self-interest or confessions because these rights were first explained as a routine element of interrogation.

Needless to say, as a matter of competent police work, this is further supported by the peace officer reducing this information to written notes at the first opportunity subsequent to the arrest.

DEFINITION: THE SERIOUS AND MINOR ARREST

These particular definitions are the ones most subject to specific local deviation and definitely require reaffirmation by further study of the governing judiciary's doctrine.

Generally, all crimes are divided into two or more classes. The more serious are regarded as felonies. Although it is possible for the peace officer to understand what constitutes a felony, achieving this comprehension can be difficult.

One can, from studying Section 335 of the United States Criminal Code, glean the belief that a felony encompasses all offenses punishable by death or imprisonment of over one year.

Further study would indicate that in most states, a felony is an offense punishable by death or confinement in a state prison or penitentiary.

However, actual unequivocal determination can only be achieved by a fairly meticulous study of applicable legislation, as in some states each offense must independently be labeled a felony in order to have this status.

Due to its rather considerable effect upon the status of the arresting peace officer, the author would recommend that police organizations provide such definitions to its members.

For the purpose of this text, an arrest for a felony will be classified as a *serious arrest* whereas all other arrests will be defined as *minor arrests.*

This distinction is applicable where we are discussing the use of force. It is not applicable, as will be shown, when discussing the use of handcuffs or the appropriateness of a search.

Insofar as safety precautions are concerned, there should be no distinction to the arresting peace officer. Each possesses an equal potential for developing into a dangerous situation. Although, to the peace officer's original knowledge, the arrest is being accomplished to satisfy a simple charge, to the suspect his knowledge of an undiscovered more severe crime will definitely influence his actions to the extent that he can present the ultimate in danger.

If this emphasis appears repetitious, it is because the author has personally experienced circumstances where two subordinates arrested a suspect on one of the simplest of all charges. Because the charge was so minor in nature no attempt was made to search the suspect but, instead, he was placed in the rear of the transporting vehicle with both policemen remaining in the front. Unfortunately, the suspect had previously committed a rape and, believing himself in serious jeopardy, produced a concealed .22-caliber automatic pistol, smaller than the average hand but big enough to fire a bullet into the back of each policeman's head.

Both policemen subsequently died as payment for this simple mistake.

In summation, the terms felony and misdemeanor, serious arrest or minor arrest are either legal or dependent upon the law for their substance. They cannot be applied as an indication of the danger involved. No type of arrest is ever sufficiently minor as to allow the peace officer, for even a moment, to lower his guard or not be constantly alert for danger.

USE OF FORCE

First, regardless of the type of arrest involved, the peace officer is normally authorized to apply that force which is necessary to protect himself. Although he can resort to the use of this type of force only as a last resort, he is *not* under the same legal obligation as that of the ordinary citizen. Usually the citizen, in order to make a plea of self-defense, other than when guarding his own property, is required to exhaust all other means of retreat before he resorts to the application of force under the guise of self-defense.

For example, when confronted by danger, the average citizen must turn and flee and only when he can no longer avail himself of escape is he justified in attacking in order to defend himself.

The policeman is not usually limited in this manner while

performing the arrest. In other words, he does not first have to retreat but instead, if, during the arrest his life is actually threatened, he can usually as a matter of course take such steps as are necessary to protect himself.

This threat cannot consist of mere declarations but must be a physical act on the part of the attacker. For example, in a minor arrest the mere fact that the suspect states, "I'm going to kill you," is usually not considered sufficient grounds for retaliatory action under the status of self-defense; but if, during the course of a minor arrest, the suspect were to produce a knife and move it in the direction of the arresting peace officer, the peace officer usually would not be required to retreat. Instead, he would normally be considered as justified in taking that action necessary to protect his own welfare.

However, those measures forthcoming for self-defense can only be sufficient to overcome the physical threat and must immediately terminate when the physical threat is no longer in existence.

Second, in both types of arrest, force is applied where possible, by the recommended procedure of first clearly indicating to the suspect exactly what is desired of him.

If the suspect refuses to comply, the order should be repeated with a warning that force will be employed.

If he still refuses, only the force necessary to overcome his resistance should be employed.

Warnings should not be repeated. Action without hesitation is essential when it becomes necessary, otherwise control of the situation will be lost.

Force should *never* be resorted to *except as a last resort* and then only the minimum applied, necessary to overcome resistance. *When actual physical resistance ceases, the peace officer immediately ceases to apply* physical force.

As in the case of self-defense, the resistance must be physical in nature. Mere threats or warnings on the part of the suspect are not usually considered sufficient to justify the use of physical force.

Again, it is reiterated, the applicability of the following procedures can only be determined by a study of the appropriately governing laws and regulations.

In a minor arrest, the force that can be applied to overcome resistance must be short of that force which could result in death. For example, an arrest for "disturbing the peace" (considered in most locales a minor arrest) would not justify the peace officer resorting to the discharge of a weapon. This type of action can and usually does result in death.

Further, justification would normally not be achieved simply because the peace officer later claims that when he shot he did not intend to kill. Any discharge of firearms is usually considered as deadly force.

All other legal elements considered satisfied, the peace officer in this type of arrest would, however, be regarded as having justification to apply a wrestling or judo hold, striking a blow with the hand, or even using his club providing his intent was clearly indicated as not attempting to critically hurt the suspect, and that the force applied was not a retaliatory vindictive measure. It can only be that force necessary to overcome resistance.

The author was present at the trial of a policeman who was charged with "aggravated assault and battery" as the result of a blow by club applied to a suspect during an arrest.

It is important to note that in this case the blow was not particularly severe, nor did it appear to have created significant injury. However, while on the witness stand, the policeman was asked why he struck the blow and his answer was, "He called me a _____ and I don't take that from nobody, so I took my club and _____."

Because, by his own testimony, the policeman clearly indicated that his intent was retaliatory in nature, he was rightfully convicted and subsequently served a considerable period in confinement. (In addition, of course, he lost his position on the police force.)

In all probability, had his intent been solely that of overcoming resistance, and had the same amount of force been applied, he would not have been considered to have committed an offense.

Where the second type of arrest, the serious arrest, is encoun-

tered, it usually is considered justifiable if the arresting peace officer resorts to the use of deadly force in overcoming resistance.
Again, it must clearly be shown that this was used only as a last
resort and where all other means had failed.

Although the courts usually consider the firing of a weapon
as deadly force, it is not considered appropriate or proper that
the peace officer must shoot to kill. Instead, as in all other measures, he resorts to the application of the minimum amount of
force necessary to overcome resistance.

Although fully aware that many police organizations prescribe
the use of a "warning" shot, the author definitely subscribes to
avoiding this practice as a means of warning.

Here we enter into a new principle. A peace officer is never
justified in jeopardizing the life of an innocent party solely as a
means of effecting an arrest. It is the opinion of the author, even
though it may not be popularly accepted, that it is better to let the
suspect escape than to jeopardize the life of an innocent bystander.
Sooner or later the suspect will be recaptured, but the dead innocent bystander can never be brought back to life.

Even though at the point of origin all signs are to the contrary,
the discharge of the firearm as a means of warning has hidden
dangers that in no way can be altogether discerned.

It is too easy to forget or disregard the tremendous power contained in a bullet's charge, the distance a bullet can travel, or its
penetrating power.

The author has investigated too many instances where the use
of a warning shot resulted in critically wounding innocent persons
not visible to the arresting officer. In one particular instance an
innocent individual was killed after the bullet had penetrated a wall
at a considerable distance from the scene of arrest. In another, an
officer riding on the running board of an automobile that swerved,
fired a shot which ricocheted, killing another officer who was a
passenger in the car.

Then, too, it is hoped that the individual engaged in police
work is physically capable of raising his voice to the extent that this
means of warning is almost as effective.

EXAMINATION

1. What is usually considered the first legal element that should be satisfied by the arresting peace officer?
2. How does the author regard the procedure of firing a warning shot? Why?
3. What is defined as a serious arrest?
4. What is regarded as a minor arrest?
5. What are the differences between the serious arrest and the minor arrest in regards to the use of handcuffs or a search?
6. When can a peace officer resort to the use of force?
7. When can the peace officer resort to the use of deadly force?
8. What type of arrest prohibits the use of any force?
9. If force is applied as a part of an arrest, when does it terminate?
10. What type of arrest requires the peace officer to take a calculated risk by jeopardizing the lives of bystanders?
11. Explain the modification to the use of force in a serious or minor arrest where the female suspect is to be arrested.

CHAPTER 4

MECHANICS OF THE SERIOUS ARREST

DISPLAY OF THE WEAPON

In the minor arrest—*the peace officer approaches the scene of the arrest with his weapon remaining in its holster.*

In the serious arrest—*the weapon is taken from the holster prior to the approach to the scene of the arrest and remains in the hand of the arresting peace officer throughout the arrest.*

Consideration is given regarding the apparent severity of this latter procedure. There is also an awareness that a few eminent authorities regard this as an unnecessary humiliation to the suspect.

Experience, however, has definitely resolved any doubts concerning the necessity of this procedure, in the mind of the author.

As was cited in describing experiences encountered in "The Horror Chamber," wherein the major number of students during the course of the indoor exercise committed mistakes resulting in their simulated deaths, practically no one failed to be simulatedly killed in a preceding exercise that was conducted out-of-doors. The primary factor that caused this so clearly supports adoption of this proposed cardinal rule that it is here described in detail as an exemplary illustration.

Keep in mind that no tension-developing elements were produced in this exercise. Instead, the elements consisted of the acting-suspect taking a stand in the middle of an empty lot. He would remain innocuous, casually throwing and catching a set of keys.

A team of students would be calmly briefed with the instructions that, in their arriving at the edge of the lot, quite some distance from the acting-suspect, they had definitely recognized him as a dangerous "wanted" person who, beyond any doubt, was known to have killed a policeman the previous day. It was further explained that they were to put into effect the techniques as cited in this text, arresting the suspect using full advantage of every safety precaution.

The particular principle emphasized was one that those who have not served in the military may have some difficulty comprehending. That is, that the range of the weapon vastly reduces distances involved. *When capturing a dangerous suspect, it is absolutely essential to immediately acquire control as soon as the range of the voice and the weapon make this feasible.*

To wait for acquisition of this control until the peace officers can proceed to the point where they can lay hands on the suspect unnecessarily exposes them to danger. Instead, the correct procedure should have been to immediately produce their weapons, cite their authoritative status, place the suspect under arrest, and require him to raise his hands. This provided immediate control of the suspect, contingent only upon a distance from which verbal communication was feasible.

The range of the weapon made actual "walking up to the suspect" unnecessary and, because it provided additional time for the suspect to plan retaliatory measures, dangerous. Failure to comprehend this was the mistake common to almost all the students, however, this is not the point in illustration.

Practically every student, even after having been warned of the inherent danger in this specific case, left his weapon remain in his holster while proceeding to walk the distance.

Meanwhile the acting-suspect eyed the uniforms of the peace officers, obviously with full knowledge of what was to occur. He continued to jangle the keys and, with what appeared to be nonchalant unconcern, dropped them. He would then casually stoop to retrieve the keys when the students were approximately a distance of six feet from him. In doing so he would, in full sight of the students, retrieve a weapon loaded with blanks which he had previously laid behind his hat and rather unhurriedly proceed to blast the students to their simulated deaths.

The students' shock can well be imagined.

The important element to consider here was that experienced and seasoned peace officers would be so stunned that they would stand frozen, apparently totally fascinated by the suspect's open movements, without ever, even in one instance, having time to remove their own weapons from their holsters.

Although the art of the "quick draw" is glamorously depicted in motion pictures and television dramas, the peace officer who has not previously taken gun in hand, and finds himself in this sort of predicament, has very little if any, chance of survival.

The suspect in this type of instance does not have to be an intellectual giant in order to fully comprehend that, sooner or later, he is going to be approached by an arresting peace officer. He usually has more than ample time to prepare for this and can easily conceal weapons in various places on his person.

The author has a particularly vivid memory of a personal experience that occurred, and further illustrates this fact. During an arrest, a number of years ago, a suspect had concealed, in the pocket of his jacket, a loaded and "cocked" German-made .38-caliber pistol. The arrest was for a charge which, although a felony, was simple in nature, and there was absolutely nothing to be gained from the suspect's appearance that would indicate any danger. During the approach it was noted that the suspect's hands were contained in his jacket pockets and, because of inclement weather, no particular attention was paid to the fact that the suspect's hands remained there while the author was satisfying the legal recitation required in the arrest. The author was brought up short by the distinct click of a hammer striking the primer of a bullet.

Only the fact that the author's weapon was in hand and pointed at the suspect's head prevented another effort at firing. Subsequent examination revealed that the suspect, holding the gun in his pocket while pointed at the author within a distance of less than two feet, had actually pulled the trigger. A defective hammer pin, and the preparation of the author altered results sufficient to allow the writing of this text. Had preparatory provision not afforded a means for the immediate use of the author's weapon, he would have been killed and the task of formulating this text would have fallen to someone else.

Let me reiterate, from the appearance of the suspect there

was absolutely no way to have prior knowledge that a gun was concealed in his pocket.

Suffice to say that the author now, unequivocally, recommends the adoption as a cardinal rule that: *in a serious arrest the weapon is to be in the hand of the peace officer, ready to shoot, prior to arriving at the scene of the arrest.*

This also brings to mind another principle that is frequently subject to controversy. That is, what occupational risks should be expected of the peace officer?

The author is fully aware that there are some calculated risks required of all individuals engaged in police work, however, he is definitely opposed to the sometimes popularly accepted school advocating the taking of unnecessary risks or the concept that, as peace officers, we are all some kind of "Hollywood heroes" subject to the philosophy expressed by the thought, "Well, those are just the chances we have to take."

There is never any justification for unnecessarily exposing a peace officer to danger. Those bent on self-extermination are best suited for other occupations, for in satisfying this hidden drive they too frequently cause the deaths of their working companions. There are already present too many unavoidable dangers without seeking the dubious category of futilely dying a hero's death.

Instead, the peace officer should unequivocally make use of every available resource: taking advantage of all possible cover; carefully preplanning; and assuring that, where available, sufficient manpower is present, prior to initiating the arrest. *The calculated risk is only justified where no other avenue is available.*

To return to the mechanics of a serious arrest, not only is the weapon in the hand of the peace officer prior to arrival but, when armed with an automatic pistol, a bullet is to be in the chamber of the weapon. Keep in mind that a distinct identifying noise is created when accomplishing this, which is discernible at quite a distance.

The safety catch is to be "on" or, not depressed. The hammer is "cocked" and rests to the rear so that, when firing is necessary, it can be accomplished simply by first depressing the safety catch and then pressing the trigger, firing "single action."

RECOMMENDED

Fig. 4. Weapon: Display of Revolver, Hammer Forward; Preparatory to be fired "double action"

In the case where the peace officer is armed with a revolver, the hammer is to rest forward, as illustrated in the figure titled: "Display of Revolver, Hammer Forward." When it is necessary to fire, it is accomplished by firing the weapon "double action."

Almost every hammerless revolver requires firing "double action," and therefore the same procedure would apply.

In both instances, during the approach the trigger finger should not be held on the trigger guard. The finger should rest on the trigger as shown in this same figure titled: "Display of Revolver, Hammer Forward."

Surprisingly, employment of this technique is more difficult to accomplish by the seasoned peace officer than by the rookie, as training has taught the seasoned officer to never place his finger on the trigger until he is ready to fire. However, adoption of this procedure is definitely recommended, as the author has witnessed too many instances where the element of surprise has caused the peace officer to "forget" and, because of situational tension, keep sqeezing the trigger guard in the hope of discharging the weapon.

In the case of the revolver, the "double action" provides the necessary safety margin. When using an automatic, training in depressing the safety catch and simultaneously squeezing of the trigger provides a smooth, uninterrupted movement and, at the same time, affords the necessary safety precaution.

The safety catch should never be depressed or "turned off" except when the gun is about to be actually fired. Failure to adhere to this principal can easily result in the shooting of an innocent person because of the unconscious human tendency to tighten the hand when startled.

In the case of the automatic, normally the weapon should be held in the right hand, even by people who are left-handed. This is so because of the position of the safety catch, however, during one phase of the search (as will be subsequently explained) the weapon is necessarily held in the left hand.

If the automatic is carried in the left hand, the thumb should not rest on the safety catch as it is too easy to drop the weapon, and even the mere discharge can "kick" it out of hand. The thumb should instead rest around the other side of the pistol grip. Where the weapon is to be fired by the left hand, the proper technique requires that the first step be to bring the thumb around the pistol grip and depress the safety catch. The next step is to bring the thumb back to its former position around the pistol grip and, almost simultaneously, squeeze the trigger. Although description sounds somewhat awkward, actual training can produce a rapid, smooth procedure.

Unless armed with a hammerless weapon, sufficient precautions should constantly be observed to avoid any obstructions in the vicinity of the hammer which could prevent the weapon from being fired either "single" or "double action."

Considering the number of unnecessary fatalities, a word

of caution is advised concerning procedures to be adopted prior to returning the weapon to the holster. In some instances it has been observed that, where the automatic pistol is used, the rookie dangerously takes a "short-cut" by easing the hammer forward without removing the cartridge from the chamber. This practice is definitely to be avoided as, when the peace officer develops this habit formation while he is calm, the movement may appear simple and dexterous; however, in the excitement of an arrest, he may perspire freely, allowing the hammer to slip from his fingers.

Instead, the weapon should be returned to the holster with the safety catch "on" and the hammer cocked to the rear. Subsequent to the arrest, when the necessity of immediate use is no longer prevalent, the peace officer should first remove the magazin, withdraw the cartridge from the chamber, and clear the weapon.

TEAMWORK

As has previously been described, the author recommends that, where possible, patrols consist of teams of peace officers. There are several factors considered in arriving at this conclusion.

First, a suspect might be tempted to resist when faced by a lone individual, but less inclined to resist when confronted by a team.

Second, the margin for mistake is considerably broadened by having two peace officers available.

Third, it is good policy to have a witness, especially if force is used.

Conversely the use of a team presents special difficulties unless previous training is applied sufficient to develop a smooth and coordinated effort.

In order to avoid the complications of disjointed efforts, one member of the team should always be previously designated as the leader or senior member of the team. Subsequently he should do most of the talking and cue the actions of the other member, or the junior member.

The senior member should not make the mistake of attempting

to accomplish all the action by himself but, instead, should delegate appropriate duties to the junior member. The junior member should very rarely, if ever, argue with regard to the course of action decided upon by the leader. He should also avoid concentrating his sight on the leader's actions but, instead—watch the suspect.

If there are two or more suspects there is a tendency for the junior member to regard the suspect with whom the leader is dealing, especially if the leader engages in conversation with one suspect. This sometimes is deliberately occasioned by the suspect to cause a diversion and allow other suspects time to produce hidden weapons. If the junior member, as illustrated in the figure titled: "Concentration on One Suspect," allows himself to be diverted from paying proper attention to the other suspects, he affords a means of successfully completing this chicanery. Instead, he allows the senior mem-

NOT RECOMMENDED
Fig. 5. Teamwork: Concentration on One Suspect

ber to deal with one suspect while he "covers" the other suspect, both by sight and his weapon.

This is especially true while the search is being accomplished and affords the senior member the means of concentrating full attention on the one suspect.

If the arrest takes place in a room, movements are always co-ordinated by the junior member automatically taking his cue from the movements of the senior member. Normally the senior member takes his stand at the extreme end of the room while the junior member responds by placing himself in the adjacent corner from the leader as illustrated in the figure titled: "Teamwork: Spread."

If the senior member moves toward the corner occupied by the junior member, the junior member moves accordingly toward the corner formerly occupied by the senior member so that the ex-change takes place simultaneously. If the leader stops, the junior

RECOMMENDED
Fig. 6. Teamwork: Spread

member stops. All movements are necessarily coordinated. This provides the most complete coverage by the spread of team members.

In the serious arrest where the weapon is displayed and it becomes necessary for one member of the team, whether senior or junior, to cross the line of fire of the other member, the member in the rear, as in figure titled: "Teamwork: Crossing Line of

RECOMMENDED

Fig. 7. Teamwork: Crossing Line of Fire

Fire," *always points his weapon up, out of range, until the other member moves out of the line of fire.*

In line with this, a word of caution concerning the holding of a weapon. Contrary to the procedure normally depicted in the movies, *the weapon is never to be used as a pointer indicating direction,* as illustrated in the figure titled: "Using Weapon as a

NOT RECOMMENDED
Fig. 8. Weapon: Using Weapon as a Pointer

Pointer." This can too easily result in an undesired firing of the weapon. Instead, the weapon never leaves the position close to the side of the peace officer, as shown in the illustration titled: "Correct Position for Carrying Weapon." It is always pointed at the suspect so that it can be fired without the necessity of changing the sight alignment.

If there is any pointing necessary, it is always accomplished by the other hand as shown in the figure titled: "Correct Method of Physically Designating Direction."

Both members of the team should concentrate their vision on the hands of the suspect. If the suspect is going to surreptitiously fire a weapon, he will not do it with his eyes. Instead, his hands should be kept in sight at all times from the very beginning of the

RECOMMENDED

Fig. 9. Weapon: Correct Position for Carrying Weapon

arrest, which, in the serious arrest, is always initiated by ordering
the suspect to raise his hands.

*Upon entering a room where a serious arrest is to be accom-
plished, action is unequivocally initiated by the senior member
covering all occupants of the room, freezing their movements, while
the junior member immediately searches all possible areas that
could hide an accomplice.*

In doing this there is to be absolutely no guesswork; bath-
rooms, closets, and even areas under beds and couches should be
thoroughly scrutinized. Only then does the junior member take
up his stance in the adjacent corner and necessary further action is
accomplished.

RECOMMENDED

Fig. 10. Weapon: Correct Method of Physically Designating Direction

MODIFICATION FOR THE MINOR ARREST

There is little to be gained by repetition of techniques previously described. Proper application of these same techniques in a minor arrest can be gained through a minor amount of study and thought. These same techniques can be easily modified for application in those phases of a minor arrest that are similar to procedures described in this and the following chapters.

EXAMINATION

1. In a serious arrest, when is the weapon taken from the holster and carried in the hand?

2. In a serious arrest, how close to the suspect does the peace officer have to get before taking control?

3. What part of the suspect should the peace officer carefully observe in order to discern a hidden weapon?

4. In a serious arrest, on what part of the suspect's anatomy should the peace officer concentrate his attention? Why?

5. What sort of risks should the peace officer accept as necessary occupational hazard?

6. In a serious arrest when armed with an automatic, when should the bullet be placed in the chamber?

7. In a serious arrest when armed with a revolver, where is the hammer and, if necessary, how is the weapon fired?

8. In a serious arrest, where does the trigger finger rest when armed with an automatic? When armed with a revolver?

9. When armed with an automatic, in which hand does the left-handed peace officer carry the automatic? Why?

10. When armed with a weapon that is not hammerless, what special precaution must be observed?

11. In teamwork, what are the special designations required prior to arrival at the arrest scene?

12. What is the applicable rule where one member of a team crosses in front of the other member, during an arrest?

13. Where there are more than one suspect, where does the junior member concentrate his attention?

14. Upon entering a room where a serious arrest is to be accomplished, what are the immediate steps to be taken?

15. What are the relative positions of the team while in a room?

16. In pointing directions during a serious arrest, what special procedures must be adopted?

17. In all minor arrests accomplished in a room, what relative positions should members of a team take?

CHAPTER 5

PRELIMINARY SEARCH

CONSIDERATIONS

During the course of routine police work the peace officer can never know in advance the previous special training or physical prowess of individuals he will be called upon to arrest.

The suspect may have received instruction in jujit-su, judo, or other devious means of self-defense.

The author recalls the many scenes of habitual offenders, who, while confined in prison, spent hours and even days meticulously teaching each other deadly blows, "breaks," and other escape devices. Yet, the peace officer is expected to engage and overcome these and all other dangerous obstacles as a normal matter of routine.

Provisions for this can only be accomplished by thorough and meticulous instruction supported by training to the extent that, no matter to what extreme the suspect resorts, his resistance will be overcome as a result of the peace officer's preparation.

As will be noted in this and other chapters, every movement, no matter how minor, has been given the maximum consideration, even to the point where it would appear that description is over-simplified. However, only where the peace officer adopts pro-cedures that never deviate from consideration of these techniques, can he have confidence that he is prepared to meet and overcome any situation that may arise.

The author is only too cognizant of his own fallibility; he bears too many scars to deny this. The requirements of a specific situa-tion or personal likes or dislikes may appropriately be used in modifying and perfecting techniques as presented here. The par-ticular value of this text, however, lies in the preconsidering of *all* of the elements involved in any circumstance together with the possible dangerous extremes that could result. Only by a study as meticulous as this, can a safe procedure be derived. Where deviations are to be adopted, they must be subjected to the acid test of "how well they hold up" under *all* of the demands that could be encountered in the most dangerous situations.

THE WALL SEARCH

It is recommended that a preliminary search be accomplished regardless of whether the arrest is a serious or minor one. Both instances require a search that should be as equally thorough. Therefore the same type of search is recommended for both instances with the only difference being that in the minor arrest the weapon remains in the holster. Even this difference does not exist if, during the course of a minor arrest, the peace officer learns that the subject is armed.

In considering the search, its added movement and exposure-time present additional complications. First, if it is not a totally thorough search, it lulls the arresting peace officer into a false sense of security. This, in turn, causes him to take more chances than if a search had not been made.

Second, it provides a longer period of exposure to possible risks and, if the arresting peace officers are not completely alert throughout, it can occasion especially dangerous possibilities.

The author is aware that throughout the field there are controversial schools of thought concerning which is the best type of search. In arriving at his final recommendation, one particular principle necessarily is considered as primary.

The ideal search contains a relationship where the suspect is kept "off-balance" throughout the search and, conversely, the arresting peace officer remains "on-balance" throughout the search.

This demand becomes absolutely imperative for those peace officers who must operate independently and cannot depend upon the protective cover which would be forthcoming had there been the support of a team member.

There is only one type of search that provides this particularly important advantage—the wall search. Therefore this text advocates this as the recommended type of search.

Although it is the safest type of search, it again is not a substitute for alertness and, of course, if not properly accomplished, its very safety factors can contribute elements of danger.

Keeping in mind that its particular advantage is that it affords the suspect's imbalance throughout the search, this goal must be actively sought for and maintained to the end of the search.

Contrary to its name, the wall search does not require a wall. Any object that can support the weight of the suspect, such as a side of a car, tree, table, or similar object, can be safely used.

The most common error is to have the suspect stand too close to the supporting object, as shown in the figure titled: "Incorrect Wall Search Position." This not only affords the suspect an "on-

NOT RECOMMENDED
Fig. 11. Search: Incorrect Wall Search Position

balance" position but, provides the use of additional muscles to assist him in an attack upon the peace officer.

By pushing against the wall and whirling on the arresting peace officer, not only is he afforded the use of his leg muscles, but he is also afforded the strength of his arm and waist muscles. This, in many cases, provides the means of attaining the speed needed to seize the peace officer and use him as a shield before either peace officer has time to adopt counter-measures, as is shown in the illustration titled: "Attack from Incorrect Wall Search Position."

NOT RECOMMENDED

Fig. 12. Search: Attack from Incorrect Wall Search Position

The correct procedure, as shown in the illustration titled: "Suspect's Correct Stance for Wall Search," entails placing the suspect's feet spread apart as far as possible and back away from the

RECOMMENDED

Fig. 13.   Search: Suspect's Correct Stance for Wall Search

wall to the distance that requires the use of his hands to keep him from falling.

There are a few individuals dexterous enough so that they can still utilize finger muscles in an effort to throw themselves back from the wall; however, the over-all danger is vastly reduced as, if this procedure is properly applied, it requires all the suspect's strength to keep himself from falling, and he is in a real "off-balance" position throughout the search.

Additional advantages can be acquired by forcing the hands as far apart as possible with the palms spread directly in contact with the wall and the fingers extended. The suspect should not be required to maintain his balance by the use of his fingertips. There are few advantages to be gained and the use of this device places an undue and cruel burden upon the suspect.

The suspect should not be allowed to arch his shoulders or buttocks, as this affords a means of quickly attaining an "on-balance" position. He should also be required to keep his head down throughout the search. The less observation he can make of the peace officer's movements, the less he is prepared to plan counter-movements.

Keeping this in mind, the peace officer when standing behind the suspect should never indicate directions by pointing. This provides an excuse for the suspect to turn his head and observe the position of the peace officer. If there are more than one suspect, all suspects should immediately be required to assume the required

NOT RECOMMENDED

Fig. 14. Search: Weapon not in Ready Position During Search

stance and remain in this position even while they are not being
searched.

As has previously been cited, in a serious arrest both peace
officers should hold their weapons in the ready position throughout the search. Although this, to a minor extent, handicaps the
movements of the searching peace officer, it provides greater
safety.

Where this is not adhered to, as is shown in the figure titled:
"Weapon Not in Ready Position During Search," it takes but a
fraction of a second for the searching officer to become so thoroughly engrossed in the search that he fails to safeguard his weapon.

Then, too, the peace officer must keep in mind that, allowing
the weapon to remain in his holster under these circumstances

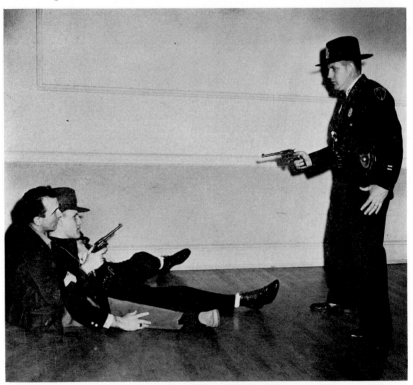

NOT RECOMMENDED

Fig. 15. Search: Result of Failure to Carry Weapon in Ready Position
During Search

affords the suspect two distinct advantages: the first, that the weapon is not as available for the peace officer's use; the second, occurs especially where the peace officer's movements place the weapon immediately adjacent to the suspect—a factor which would not have occurred if the weapon were retained in the peace officer's hand.

To the person well-versed in the art of judo, the "break" for the wall search would be a sidewise tumble. Where the peace officer is available because of his location, a judo expert not only makes use of the judo tumble, but can utilize the body of the peace officer as a fulcrum, gaining access to the weapon during the fall with the end result as illustrated in the figure titled: "Result of Failure to Carry Weapon in Ready Position During Search."

RECOMMENDED

Fig. 16. Search: Wall Search; Imaginary Line Dividing Areas to be Searched

Added to all this, even if during the course of the search the suspect is able to grab the peace officer, he, in turn, is afforded the means of warding off the suspect with his free hand while shooting with the hand holding the weapon. This can be accomplished, even after being thrown and falling to the ground.

These elements, again, are particularly important in those instances where the peace officer is alone and cannot rely upon the efforts of an accompanying peace officer for rectification of his own errors.

In fulfilling the correct procedure the next required step entails the searching peace officer to visualize a mental image whereby an imaginary line, as illustrated in the figure titled: "Wall Search; Imaginary Line Dividing Areas to be Searched," is drawn down the center of the suspect's back.

NOT RECOMMENDED
Fig. 17. Search: Loss of Balance Due to Crossing Imaginary Division

He must keep this image in mind throughout the entire transaction and never search past or reach across this imaginary line. Failure to do so, as is illustrated in the figure titled: "Loss of Balance Due to Crossing Imaginary Division," causes the loss of the primary advantage afforded by the wall search—the "on-balance" position of the searching peace officer. It can also result in the suspect's successful application of a wrestling or judo hold.

If there are more than one suspect, the maximum safety is achieved by having the one suspect to be searched take up a position at a distance from the other suspects. The junior member covers all suspects not being searched while the senior member searches both sides of the one suspect in the manner to be described. Relative positions are as illustrated in the figure titled: "Correct Wall Search, Positions of More Than One Suspect."

RECOMMENDED

Fig. 18. Search: Correct Wall Search, Positions of More than One Suspect

The junior member remains stationary until all movements to accomplish the search of the one suspect are completed by the senior member. The junior member's position is at that end of the line adjacent to the searching peace officer as this provides a means of avoiding the senior member from coming into his range where it is necessary to fire.

Where a lone peace officer encounters more than one suspect, he is placed in a precarious position at this point, particularly if the suspects are dangerous. Decision as to resolution is dependent to a great extent upon circumstances. If he is in a crowded, well-populated area, he can keep his suspects in the wall position with the hope that a passerby will accomplish the necessary action to secure additional help; or he can dispense with the search, secure the hands of the suspects either by handcuffs or their belts and proceed with them to the station house.

The reasoning behind advocating dispensing with the search is that, if the independent peace officer attempts to make the search prior to the application of restraining devices, it is too easy for him to become engrossed in the one suspect being searched, affording the unrestrained suspects an opportunity to make use of hidden weapons.

There are several obstacles considerably handicapping attempts to make the search after the suspects are handcuffed. In order to secure the advantages of a wall search, the suspect's hands would have to be handcuffed with his hands in front (a practice the author never condones, as will be explained further).

If, instead, the hands are restrained behind the suspect, the use of the head prohibits keeping the suspect in the wall search position for periods other than of extremely short duration, as to do so requires muscular strains that are either impossible or extremely torturous.

Therefore, the search would have to be accomplished while the suspect remains in a standing position. Even though he is handcuffed with his hands behind him, it can become possible that he then has access to a hidden weapon. He can also make use of his feet, a practice that some individuals have been able to develop to a level of extreme dexterity.

This, then, makes concentration on the search by the peace officer extremely dangerous to the point where it is better to dispense with it altogether.

A third avenue remains for those who have recourse for seeking additional police aid by means of radio communication. Keeping in mind that by taking full advantage of the range of the weapon the peace officer has fairly free movement in gaining access to his transmitter while still maintaining adequate "cover" of his suspects.

Even where the peace officer is fortunate enough to be part of a team there are several special precautions that should be adopted under these circumstances.

Whenever a suspect is to be moved from one position on the wall to another, both peace officers step back, well away from the suspects. Only one suspect is to be allowed to move at a time.

The one suspect should be moved to the searching position, searched, hands secured, and then moved back into line. *All suspects should be required to keep their heads down* with the peace officers not providing an excuse for deviation by indicating directions other than through the use of verbal instructions. *All suspects should be strictly prohibited from exchanging conversation.*

If these cardinal rules are rigidly adhered to, two officers can safely search a comparatively large number of dangerous suspects.

The most common error encountered in this procedure is where the junior member fails to concentrate on guarding his allocated prisoners, but is instead diverted by watching the movements of the senior member.

It is again reiterated that it takes only a fraction of a second of inattention to provide a means for a suspect to gain control of the situation.

Where there is only one suspect, the senior member takes his position on one side of the suspect while the junior member always places himself on the other side, as is illustrated in the figure titled: "Wall Search; Correct Police Positions."

Where it becomes necessary, in order to avoid crossing the imaginary line of division, for the senior member to move over to the other side of the suspect, the junior member accordingly moves

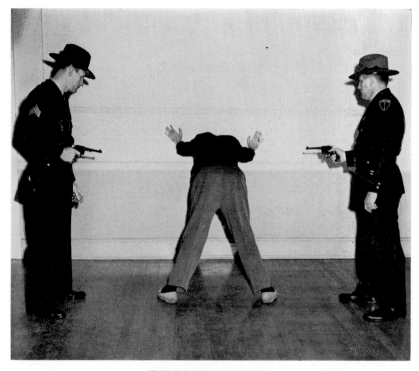

RECOMMENDED
Fig. 19. Search: Wall Search; Correct Police Positions

to the side vacated by the senior member, both peace officers keeping in mind the rule of raising the pistol when one crosses in line of fire of the other.

Again, this warning may sound repetitious, especially in view of its simplicity; however, the author recalls an incident that required investigation which originally appeared to be the murder of one member of a police team by a suspect.

Both the suspect and the two arresting peace officers were foreign nationals and initial perusary examination indicated that the suspect had produced a hidden weapon, shot and killed one peace officer, and thrown his weapon on the ground while the other peace officer fired unsuccessfully, allowing the suspect to escape.

Unfortunately, ballistic tests and angles of entry unequivocally proved that the suspect had simply fired the gun straight up in the air, causing the second peace officer a sufficient startle reaction that, without thinking, he squeezed the trigger of his own weapon which happened to be pointed at the back of his team partner, killing him instantly.

In order to be thorough, the search must be accomplished in a systematic manner. Training should develop a routine procedure from which there is never deviation. The searching peace officer's first step is to remove the suspect's hat, carefully examine it by probing, and drop it to the ground. Next the palm, of the one hand on the side adjacent to the searching peace officer, is removed from the wall and the areas between the fingers are examined as is illustrated in the figure titled: "Examination of Palm."

Lest the reader be deceived by the impression that description of this step is over-simplified, consider that the author has witnessed innumerable students, in heat of anxiety created by tension, who

RECOMMENDED
Fig. 20. Search: Examination of Palm

have totally ignored a suspect holding a switch-blade knife flat against the wall by pressing with his outstretched palm.

There are several simple principles that should be adhered to throughout the search. The searching peace officer facing the side of the suspect always uses his hand nearest the wall for the searching process. Thus, when he searches the right side of the supect, compliance with this rule causes him to use his right hand for the search. When he searches the left side of the suspect, he uses his left hand.

Accordingly, the weapon is held in the hand fartherest from the wall. Thus the peace officer holds his weapon in his left hand while searching the right side of the suspect. (This is the only time the weapon is held in the left hand.) This, of course, keeps the searching peace officer's weapon at as far a distance from the suspect as possible, and affords the use of the other hand as a means of warding off, if the suspect attacks.

The searching peace officer utilizes his foot nearest the wall to engage the suspect's foot. This engagement should not occur until after considering the relative size of the suspect in comparison to the peace officer and the peace officer has proceeded that far down the side of the suspect to the point where he can accomplish engaging the foot without throwing himself "off-balance."

Engaging the suspect's foot should be accomplished by the peace officer placing his ankle bone as tight against the suspect's ankle bone as is possible. When this is accomplished, the searcher is afforded a means whereby, through his ankle bone, he can feel major movement made by any other part of the suspect's anatomy.

In addition, where the searcher keeps his other foot well back and squarely on the ground, if he feels any movement he can, simply by stepping back, throw the suspect completely "off-balance" by slight pressure against the suspect's foot.

When the clothing is examined, the hand should not slide over the clothes, nor should they be patted. Flat objects will remain undiscovered if this is done. Instead, a cardinal rule is that *every inch of the clothing should*, as illustrated in the figure titled: "Crushing Clothing," *be grasped in the hand and actually crushed*. If this is properly done, when the search is completed,

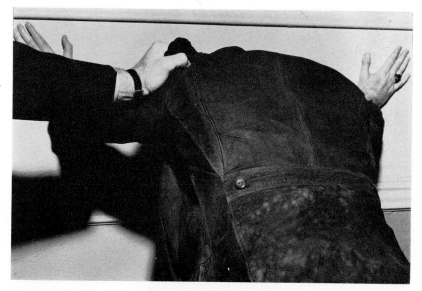

RECOMMENDED
Fig. 21. Search: Crushing Clothing

there is little doubt concerning the suspect's still retaining a hidden weapon.

After searching the palm, the senior member then proceeds to search the cuff, sleeve, and—by inserting his fingers—the collar of the shirt, jacket and coat. The same crushing procedure is accomplished over the entire area above the waistline of the one side. The belt is then searched in a manner similar to that used with the collar, whereby the hand is definitely inserted and every inch is carefully crushed.

He then proceeds to the area below the waistline, always staying inside of the imaginary dividing line and, as illustrated in the figure titled: "Proper Crouching Position for Wall Search," he does not bend over when searching the lower half; instead, he assumes a balanced crouch. This retains his ability to pull the suspect's foot, if necessary, and prohibits his arriving at an "off-balance" position.

The senior member continues down the body of the suspect, meticulously examining every inch, including the crotch, cuffs of

RECOMMENDED

Fig. 22. Search: Proper Crouching Position for Wall Search

the trousers and, by insertion of his fingers, the inside area of the shoe and sock, working completely around the foot to assure that no area is left unsearched.

The leader then, as illustrated in the figure titled: "Examination of the Shoe Bottom," steps back and away from the suspect and instructs the suspect to raise his foot. Holding the foot, the senior member carefully scrutinizes the sole, paying particular attention to the area immediately adjacent to the heel.

The senior member, having completed the search on one side, moves to the other side with the junior member responding accordingly and, the same procedure is put into effect accomplishing the search on the other side.

Total application of procedures described provide the maximum safety and thoroughness; however, these advantages can only

RECOMMENDED

Fig. 23. Search: Examination of the Shoe Bottom for Wall Search

be achieved where every described technique is rigidly adhered to. Carelessness at any point completely nullifies every other precaution.

The suspect is then ready to be handcuffed.

OTHER TYPES OF SEARCH

As has previously been stated, other types of search are predominantly advocated by a few eminent police schools. Certainly it is not the intention of this text to prescribe the only applicable answer.

Where preferences for these other types of search exist, many of the procedures described—such as "crushing" the clothing, systematic search, imaginary division of the body, and teamwork movements—are applicable and will greatly enhance any type of search.

Here we will present the various types of search, but from a negative viewpoint, primarily to explain their weaknesses and dangerous traits.

It is to be noted that in none of these searches is the advantageous relationship achieved whereby the searching peace officer remains "on-balance" and the suspect remains "off-balance" throughout the entire search. This has previously been stated as a major loss, however, detailed examination should provide an even better appreciation.

NOT RECOMMENDED

Fig. 24. Search: Position of Suspect for Standing Search

STANDING SEARCH

This type of search is most frequently resorted to but unfortunately its only advantage is that it provides a "short cut." This, of course, is of questionable value. Although it takes little or no time to have the suspect get into the required stance, as illustrated in the figure titled: "Position of Suspect for Standing Search," other than having the suspect raise his hands, it provides no advantages for the searching peace officer.

The mere fact that the suspect raises his hands can increase the dangers to the peace officer for, as is illustrated in the figure titled: "Search: by the Peace Officer in the Standing Search," the suspect is in a perfect preparatory position to strike a blow, particularly a deadening judo "chop."

NOT RECOMMENDED

Fig. 25. Search: by the Peace Officer in the Standing Search

The suspect has the advantage of being able to completely observe all movements of the peace officer throughout the search. Should the peace officer, in concentrating too much upon the search, fail to be aware of the movements of the suspect, for even a fraction of a second, he is extremely vulnerable to having his weapon taken from him. Even where he is afforded the additional margin of safety by being accompanied by another team member, the suspect, without any particular agility, can fairly easily grab him and use him as a shield nullifying this additional support.

Even though the suspect's legs are spread apart, he still retains advantage of foot movements which can become dangerous weapons. During this type of search the peace officer can engage his foot inside of the suspect's foot; however, regardless of how far apart the suspect's feet are spread, he still remains sufficiently "on-balance" that it becomes very difficult, if not at times impossible, to "throw him" by this means. In fact, the whole act of engaging his foot becomes questionable. Particularly from a speculative examination, it is possible that the peace officer could, if circumstances so warrant, kick the suspect's foot out from under him. The drawback, however, is that the suspect can almost as easily kick the peace officer's foot out from under him.

Finally, the suspect remains "on-balance" throughout the search while, during certain phases of the search, the peace officer borders close to an "off-balance" position.

KNEELING SEARCH

As is illustrated in the figure titled: "Position of the Suspect in the Kneeling Search," in this type of search the suspect remains on the ground with his hands raised above his head. Although, of the three types of searches not recommended, this type is the most advantageous because it, to some extent, immobilizes the feet of the suspect, it has very few more benefits than the "standing" search.

In this type of search the suspect again remains "on-balance," throughout the search while the peace officer is even more "off-

NOT RECOMMENDED
Fig. 26. Search: Position of the Suspect in the Kneeling Search

balance," as illustrated in the figure titled: "Search: by the Peace Officer in the Kneeling Search."

Where this type of search is advocated, frequently the suspect is required to clasp his hands behind his head. In a suspect's attack the advantages of this are extremely dubious as, with the hands extended above the head, the movement of the hands is more quickly discernable.

While searching the lower front part of the suspect the peace officer is extremely vulnerable, and a distinct disadvantage of this search is that examination of the knees and front part of the lower extremities becomes almost impossible.

NOT RECOMMENDED

Fig. 27.   Search: by the Peace Officer in the Kneeling Search

PRONE SEARCH

The prone search superficially appears to be the safest type of search, however, of all the searches it presents the most inherent dangers. In this type of search the suspect lies flat on the ground as illustrated in the figure titled: "Position of the Suspect in the Prone Search," arms and feet extended. The suspect can be made to lie with his face pointed directly to the ground, however, he is not required to move his head very far in order for him to have total observation of all the peace officer's movements.

Contrary to appearances, the experienced wrestler is quick to recognize that the suspect is in a definite "on-balance" position, where he has full advantage of free movement of either his hands or legs. While conversely, as illustrated in the figure titled: "Search

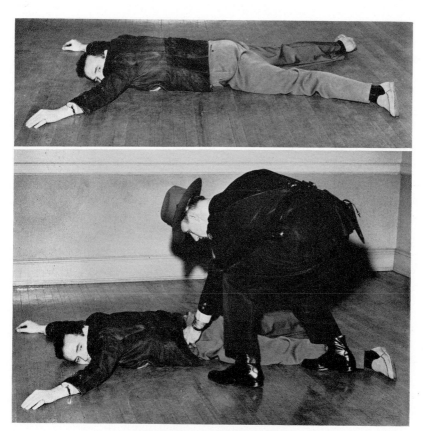

NOT RECOMMENDED

Fig. 28. Search: Position of the Suspect in the Prone Search

NOT RECOMMENDED

Fig. 29. Search: by the Peace Officer in the Prone Search

by the Peace Officer in the Prone Search," the peace officer is definitely "off-balance," throughout the search.

In this type of search a well aimed kick can totally render the peace officer incapable of further resistance.

In an effort to offset the inherent dangers of this, the practice of having the peace officer seek recourse to kneeling while making the search is frequently advocated. Although this provides the peace officer with a better "on-balance" position, it definitely hampers his movement and can prove particularly deadly where he is subject to attack. The suspect, by a half-roll, body twist and kick, can move fast enough with a minor degree of agility that the kneeling peace officer is unable to move out of line of the attack.

Naturally no means is afforded to "throw" the suspect, as he is already on the ground.

Finally, the peace officer has his choice between two particular dangers. He can disregard searching the front of the suspect, as the suspect's body pressing the ground prohibits a thorough search of this part of his clothing from this position, however, if he does he might as well have not made a search; or, he can turn the suspect over and, while the suspect is lying on his back, attempt to complete the search.

This requires some rather foolhardy chances, as the position of the peace officer is already bent in an "off-balance" position. A very slight yank by the suspect can finish the indicated direction and, in addition, if the suspect has any knowledge of wrestling or judo, the use of the knee provides a remarkably effective "throw."

Even coming close to the suspect makes the peace officer extremely vulnerable as the target of a deadly kick.

CULMINATIVE EFFECTS

If the peace officer is primarily concerned with the comfort of the suspect, then the three "not recommended" types of search are properly in order. For, in assuming the stance necessary in the "wall search," somewhat of a strain is placed upon the muscles of the suspect.

It is definitely not recommended that this be the criteria as a form of punishment for the suspect; however, it does have its advantages in that the tiring effect lessens the suspect's ability to render an attack.

Because of this, the search should be accomplished as expeditiously as is feasible. In the other three types of search the suspect remains comfortable throughout the search and no particular speed is required.

EXAMINATION

1. What signs does the peace officer look for to recognize the "black belt" judo expert?
2. What are the only means afforded the peace officer in overcoming the judo expert or wrestler?
3. Which of the four types of search is the recommended type of search?
4. In the wall search, what type of wall is mandatorily required?
5. Name five distinct advantages provided solely by the wall search.
6. In the wall search, what particular danger is presented if the suspect is not required to assume the proper stance?
7. What factors regarding the suspect's feet should be accomplished in the wall search?
8. During the wall search, what important principle should the peace officer remember when giving directions?
9. When there is more than one suspect, when are those suspects not being searched required to assume the wall search stance?
10. (a) What is the recommended position of the weapon during the search after a serious arrest?
    (b) After a minor arrest?
    (c) After a minor arrest where the suspect is known to be armed and dangerous?
11. Where there is more than one suspect to be searched, state one of the cardinal rules concerning the movement of suspects.
12. How does the peace officer avoid searching that part of the suspect's body that would cause the peace officer to get into an "off-balance" position?
13. Where the lone peace officer arrests more than one suspect, cite two of the three recommended procedures regarding the search.
14. In citing the peace officer's techniques used during the search, which hand does the searching and which foot engages the suspect's foot?
15. Where there is a team, in searching the right side of the suspect, on which side does the junior member stand? When they

are searching the left side, on which side does the junior member stand?

16. What is the first article of the suspect's clothing that is searched?

17. What is the first part of the suspect's body that is searched?

18. What is the last part of the suspect that is searched?

19. When is the only occasion that the peace officer holds his weapon in his left hand?

20. When is the only time during the search that the two peace officers take up positions adjacent to each other?

21. In engaging the suspect's foot during the search, why is special consideration given to the ankle bone?

22. What part of the suspect's clothing should be searched by the "hard press, sliding movement?"

23. What is the recommended procedure for searching the area around the foot of the suspect?

24. What special procedure is recommended regarding the searching of collars, belts and cuffs?

25. Is it considered proper to search the suspect's crotch?

26. In searching the sole of the shoe, what special procedure is recommended?

27. What is the sole advantage of the standing search?

28. Of all the types of search, which type does the author say appears the safest and yet is the most dangerous?

29. In regards to the suspect clasping his hands behind his head, what advantages are cited by the author?

CHAPTER 6

THE USE OF RESTRAINING DEVICES

WHEN USED

The controversy regarding when handcuffs should be used has extended even into legal argument. In many instances peace officers have been accused of unnecessary brutality, both by the law and by their own organizations where they applied handcuffs.

The particular paradox is the fact that, after the handcuffs were applied, the suspect offered no resistance and was later defined as a peaceable citizen who had no intent of resisting. Whether originally the suspect had such intent is an unanswerable question.

This controversy is particularly acute where dealing with juveniles and yet, as a whole, the juvenile is more prone to an impulsive acting-out without total thought to consequences than any other type of offender.

As with all other preventative means described in this text, certainly where the peace officer fails to take necessary safety precautions, thereby tempting the suspect to a "chance" attack which ultimately results in the suspect being seriously injured or even killed, the total effect is a far cry from kindness to the suspect.

Where applied properly, the handcuff offers little if any discomfort, even if the suspect's hands are bound behind him. There is no comparison to the discomfort caused by the retaliatory measures resulting when an unsuccessful attack is made by the suspect. In the event that the reader has never been shot, it can without difficulty be accepted that, even if the recipient is not critically wounded, recovery is usually a long, painful experience.

In argument that by handcuffing a suspect, he is subjected to unnecessary humiliation, has no more logic than other arguments advanced by expostulators against this practice. The suspect, handcuffed or not, should never be exposed to public view unless it is absolutely unavoidable. The fact that a suspect is paraded in public between two peace officers is humiliating whether or not he is handcuffed.

In summation, the author advocates as a cardinal rule that: *recourse to the use of handcuffs should be left entirely to the discretion of the arresting peace officer.* Its use should not be dependent upon the nature of the charge (such as serious or minor arrest), nor the area where the arrest is made, as its effectiveness is totally dependent upon the intent of the suspect.

This intent remains invisible in the mind of the suspect and only the peace officer, at the scene of the arrest, is in a position where, by observation, he is best suited for logical determination.

ERRORS IN USE

After the search is completed there is a mistaken tendency for the peace officer to relax, assuming that the most dangerous aspects of the arrest have been completed. This is definitely not so. The only time that the dangerous aspects have been completed is when the suspect is safely behind bars.

If, however, the arresting peace officer does momentarily commit this mistake and, as a result, becomes careless in applying the handcuffs, his previous safety measures can easily have been futile.

If anything the danger increases, as frequently the suspect is finally confronted with the full realization that reliance upon hidden weapons can no longer be successful. Even where weapons were not hidden, the suspect is undeniably faced with the fact that the application of handcuffs swiftly brings to a close the period where he can escape. If latent intentions to escape were present, there is a tendency at this point for them to be overtly acted upon. Therefore the peace officer must be even more alert and again rely upon previous training for the application of systematic procedures that prohibit the opportunity arising for the suspect's escape.

Handcuffs provide a remarkable preventative measure assuring the safety of both the peace officer and the suspect, if they are applied properly.

Contrary to the procedure of application frequently depicted in the movies or on television, an unopened handcuff should never be applied by snapping it against the wrist of the suspect. Even where they are not "double locked" they can cause serious lacerations to the skin. If the peace officer should "forget" and the "jaw" of the handcuff not swing free or be "double locked," he can very easily cause a fracture of one of the many small bones contained in the suspect's wrist.

The recommended procedure therefore, as illustrated in the figure titled: "Proper Application of Open Handcuff," is to always open the "jaw" of the handcuff before the handcuff is applied.

Handcuffs should never be closed so tight that the flow of blood is obstructed. When hand cuffs are closed too tightly, they

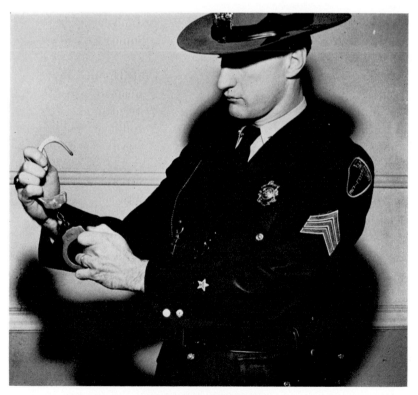

RECOMMENDED
Fig. 30. Restraint: Proper Application of Open Handcuff

cause the bones of the wrist in turn to close off the blood vessels. This in turn causes swelling which, in a short time, can produce disastrous medical results.

With it there frequently occurs a counter-charge against the peace officer that can be equally as disastrous.

When knighthood was prevalent, before the use of firearms, there was a particularly popular weapon that consisted of a ball with chain attached to a spike. The inertia of the free swinging ball was usually sufficient to break through the heaviest armor made.

Where the peace officer attaches one handcuff and allows the other to swing freely, he provides the suspect with an as equally dangerous weapon. Its effect upon the skull of a peace officer is strikingly similar to that produced upon armor in days of old. Therefore, a cardinal rule is: *where one handcuff is applied, the other handcuff is to be held firmly by the peace officer.*

Even this does not accomplish the ultimate in safety. It is hoped that here, again, procedures normally depicted in the movies or on television are not as popularly advocated in efficient police organizations.

The most glaring error is where the peace officer leads the suspect by holding on to the unattached bracelet. This, in itself, is not so particularly dangerous; however, considering the human element, it is too easy to imagine that the peace officer, in reaching for an object, forgets and lets go of the unattached bracelet leaving himself in an extremely precarious position.

In line with this, there is no particular advantage to be gained by attaching one bracelet to the wrist of the peace officer while the other remains attached to the wrist of the suspect.

Possibly this prevents the suspect from escaping without taking the person of the peace officer with him. Unfortunately, as unbelievable as it sounds, the author has been subjected to the particularly humiliating experience of having a subordinate peace officer dragged three miles away from his destination by a "hopped up" suspect.

The fact that the suspect's strength was, in the main, derived as a result of the use of cocaine did little to allay the abashed feelings of the subordinate. As if the experience itself was not bad enough, this particular peace officer held a position of responsibility requiring his leadership of a fairly large number of personnel.

Even where this extreme is not accomplished, it is too easy for a suspect, though weighing a great deal less than the peace officer, to use his foot as a fulcrum and "jerk" the peace officer completely "off-balance."

Finally, in considering what should not be done with handcuffs, the author strongly recommends against the practice of applying the handcuffs with the suspect's hands in front of him. This, of course, aids the suspect's movements, such as getting in and out of automobiles, and opening doors; but, if the peace officer were foolish enough to present the suspect with a pair of "brass knuckles," he would offer him no more additional advantages than fastening the handcuffs in this manner.

When the handcuffs are raised above the suspect's head and brought down sharply, the handcuffs provide an extremely effective cutting device in separating skin, scalp, etc.

In summation, the author unequivocally recommends that, where the handcuffs are applied, regardless of how serious the nature of the charge; they always be used to fasten *the suspect's hands behind him*. In particularly dangerous cases additional immobilization can be accomplished by running the suspect's trouser belt over the links between the bracelets of the handcuffs. Movements in mounting and dismounting automobiles can be facilitated by assisting the suspect.

The application of handcuffs can present additional dangers because, again, the peace officer can be lulled into a false sense of security that this restraint totally precludes an attack from the suspect.

Almost all handcuffs contain devices affording what is termed "single locking" and "double locking." The three types most commonly manufactured are herein described.

In the one usually referred to as the "H & R Type," the handcuff is distinct from any other type of handcuff, being much larger and accordingly, much more effective. In this type of handcuff the key has an exceptionally long stem and is terminated by two prongs. It is inserted into the handle of the bracelet; however, in order to accomplish this, the link must be moved aside so that the inside "knuckle" clears the key hole. To unlock this type of handcuff, the key is turned clockwise. To "double lock" this kind of handcuff the key is turned "counter-clockwise."

In the second type of handcuff and the one most popularly used, recognition is afforded by the fact that the key has a small additional prong at the top of the knob. Examination of the stem of the bracelet will reveal a small hole. "Double locking" is accomplished by inserting the prong in this hole. Where this type of handcuff has not been "double locked," it is opened by turning the key "clockwise." Where it has been "double locked," the key is first turned "counter-clockwise" until a distinct "click" is felt, then it is turned "clockwise" until the "jaw" springs free.

The third type of handcuffs, which appears the same as the latter type, can be distinguished by the absence of the prong on the key. "Double locking" is accomplished by turning the key "counter clockwise."

There are other variations not frequently encountered, for example, the author has in his possession a set of handcuffs manufactured in Japan wherein "double locking" is achieved by the movement of a small lever on the face of the handcuff's stem; however, "double locking" in this case is almost totally ineffective because of its availability to the suspect.

"Single locking" is always accomplished simply by inserting the "jaw" into the stem where the opposite teeth automatically engage because of a spring device.

Determination as to whether handcuffs are "double locked" or not is easily accomplished by examining the movement of the "jaw" of the handcuff. Where the "jaw" is "frozen" and cannot be moved in either direction, the handcuff is "double locked." Where the "jaw" after being engaged can only be moved in one direction, it is "single locked."

A cardinal rule that must be adopted is that *where the handcuffs are applied, they must always be "double locked."*

There are several reasons for this. The most important one can best be illustrated by citing the experience of the author who, it must be emphasized, is not particularly dexterous. But during the years of teaching this subject he was able, with the aid of a paper clip, to remove handcuffs fastened behind his back, while being timed by the class, within a two minute period.

No particularly complex procedure was developed in order to do this, instead it was accomplished by simply laying a portion of the unbent wire from the paper clip on top of the teeth of the "jaw", pressing the "jaw" until the paper clip locked the opposite engaging teeth, and then pulling out the "jaw." Needless to say, this cannot be accomplished if the handcuffs are "double locked."

Even when the handcuffs are "double locked," they can be "picked" open. The H & R handcuffs present the most obstacles against this, however, "picking" the handcuffs becomes decidedly more difficult where the handcuffs are "double locked."

In addition where the handcuffs are "single locked," an accidental hard blow can too easily cause them to tighten with the sometimes disastrous consequences of interrupting the normal blood flow in the wrists.

SUBSTITUTE RESTRAINING DEVICES

Frequently, because of the number of suspects or other circumstances, the peace officer must seek recourse to the adoption of substitutive measures in place of handcuffs. The most feasible means of accomplishing this is to use the suspect's trouser belt or necktie. There are some elements that should be given consideration so as to achieve the maximum effectiveness.

Where the necktie is used, it should not in one loop encircle both wrists as illustrated in the figure titled: "Improper Use of Necktie as a Restraining Device." This method allows the suspect the use of his biceps to stretch and loosen the encircling loop, frequently affording him the means of throwing off its restraint.

Instead, *where a substitutive restraining device is resorted to, there should be a separate loop provided for each wrist,* as illustrated in the figure titled: "Correct Use of Necktie as a Restraining Device," which is terminated by a knot. The link between the wrists should be of extremely short length; thus prohibiting the use of the thumb and fingers in untying the knots.

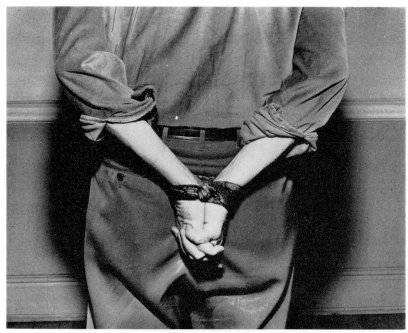

NOT RECOMMENDED
Fig. 31. Restraint: Improper Use of Necktie as Restraining Device

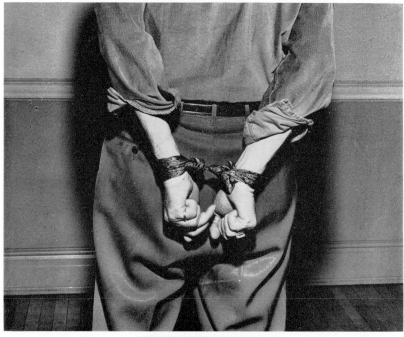

RECOMMENDED
Fig. 32. Restraint: Correct Use of Necktie as a Restraining Device

TECHNIQUES OF APPLICATION

After completion of the search and while the suspect remains in the wall position, the same stance of the suspect is utilized for the application of the handcuffs.

In the event that the suspect is not in this stance, in order to achieve the ultimate in safety precautions, he should be required to assume this position.

As the completed search provides a fairly safe assumption that the suspect no longer possesses any hidden weapons, and during the course of attaching the handcuffs the peace officer remains back away from the suspect—vastly reducing his ability to surreptitiously grab the weapon—the peace officer returns the weapon to the holster.

Failure to do so reduces the application of the handcuffs to

NOT RECOMMENDED

Fig. 33. Restraint: Application of Handcuffs with Weapon in Hand

an extremely awkward procedure. Proper application requires the use of both of the peace officer's hands. Where the peace officer retains weapon in hand, as is illustrated in the figure titled: "Application of Handcuffs with Weapon in Hand," the danger is too prevalent that the weapon might be accidentally discharged.

The peace officer takes up a position directly behind the suspect with handcuffs in hand and the "jaw" open, preparatory to encircling the wrist of the suspect.

The most common error encountered at this point is where the peace officer leans forward around the body of the suspect in an eager effort to assist him in bringing his hand to the rear. This, as is shown in the illustration titled: "Unnecessary Exposure during Application of Handcuffs," is not only a totally useless move

NOT RECOMMENDED

Fig. 34. Restraint: Unnecessary Exposure during Application of Handcuffs

but, in addition, places the peace officer in a rather perfect position for a judo "throw."

Instead, the peace officer should remain stationary until each command has been completely complied with. No movement should extend past the middle of the lower part of the suspect's back. Each movement should be definite and the peace officer should not proceed to the next step until each step is totally completed.

The first order in application should be: "Take your right hand off the wall and place it in the small of your back." The peace officer, as is illustrated in the figure titled: "Hand of Suspect in the Middle of His Back," carefully observes the position of the

RECOMMENDED

Fig. 35. Restraint: First Step in the Application of Handcuffs;
Hand of Suspect in the Middle of His Back

suspect to assure that the left hand is needed to support the weight of the suspect and that the right hand is bent and placed in the small of the back.

When this is accomplished, he takes a slight step forward, fastens the cuff so that the key hole is readily accessible, and determines that the bracelet is tight enough to prevent its being slipped over the hand, yet not that tight to the degree where it would stifle the blood flow. When these requirements are ascertained, the peace officer "double locks" the right bracelet.

After this entire order has been executed the peace officer firmly holding the left bracelet steps slightly back and instructs the suspect, "Move up and put your head against the wall." The suspect should be allowed to move slightly forward, however, it

RECOMMENDED

Fig. 36. Restraint: Second Step in the Application of Handcuffs;
Position with Head Against Wall

should be determined that he still requires the use of the muscles in his neck and feet in order to support his position. The feet should still remain well back away from the wall and spread far apart, as illustrated in the figure titled: "Position with Head Against the Wall."

The peace officer is then ready to proceed to his next order which is: "Take your left hand off the wall and place it in the small of your back." He applies the left bracelet in the manner as illustrated in the figure titled: "Fastening the Second Hand-cuff." The same elements cited for the application of the bracelet to the right hand are here repeated. Again the peace officer culminates this movement by "double locking" the handcuff.

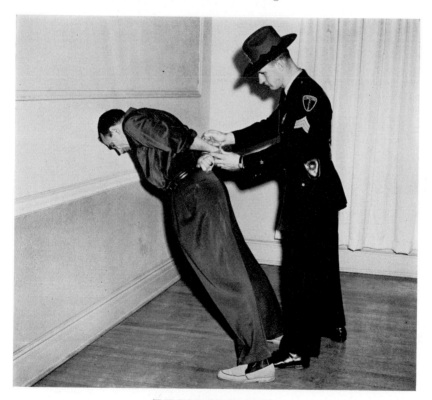

RECOMMENDED

Fig. 37. Restraint: Third Step in the Application of Handcuffs;
Fastening the Second Handcuff

The peace officer is then ready to proceed to the fourth and final step which is to order the suspect, "Stand up and face the wall." If the suspect has been in the proper position, it will be necessary to help him to do this. The suspect is now safely handcuffed, as is illustrated in the figure titled: "Suspect Properly Secured Remains Facing the Wall."

RECOMMENDED

Fig. 38. Restraint: Fourth and Final Step in the Application of Handcuffs; Suspect Properly Secured Remains Facing Wall

Where the tie or belt is used to secure the suspect, individual movements to tie each hand are accomplished in much the same manner.

Where there are more than two suspects, instead of the peace officer changing positions, the peace officers at this point back well away from the suspects, order the secured suspect to back away from the wall, join the other end of the line of suspects, and move the next suspect into position for search.

EXAMINATION

1. What particular discomfort is the suspect subject to when handcuffed?
2. Why does the author declare that handcuffing a suspect is not particularly humiliating?
3. What cardinal rule does the author advocate as the basis for determining when handcuffs should be used?
4. On which wrist is the handcuff first snapped on?
5. How tight or how loose should the applied handcuff be?
6. What is the advantage of attaching one handcuff to the suspect and allowing the other to swing freely?
7. What is the advantage of attaching the handcuffs to the suspect's hands while in front of him?
8. What is the advantage of attaching one handcuff to the wrist of the suspect and the other to the wrist of the peace officer?
9. What is the cardinal rule regarding the position of the suspect's hands when they are handcuffed?
10. When handcuffs are applied, what is the cardinal rule concerning "locking" them?
11. Where the handcuffs have an accompanying key with a prong at the top of the knob, what is indicated?
12. Where this type of handcuff has been "double locked," how is it unlocked?
13. By examining the "jaw" of the handcuff, how can it be determined whether or not the handcuff is "single locked?"
14. Is it easier to "pick" handcuffs that are "single locked" or "double locked"?
15. Where the suspect's necktie is used as a substitute restraining device, what cardinal rule should be considered?
16. What position should the suspect be in for the safest application of handcuffs?
17. Where does the peace officer's weapon rest during the application of handcuffs?

18. Give the four verbal orders required in executing the application of handcuffs.
19. Give the four verbal orders necessary for application of a substitutive restraining device.
20. When there are more than one suspect, when is each suspect handcuffed?

CHAPTER 7

TRANSPORTING THE SUSPECT AND HIS COMPLETE SEARCH

THE "FOLLOW THROUGH"

After the suspect has been carefully searched and secured by the use of a proper restraining device, he still represents a threat. Granted, realization of this occurring is vastly reduced, however, if the arresting peace officer at any time grows careless, the odds against him acutely rise.

The most common error encountered is where the senior member fails to continually scrutinize the movements of the suspect. Again, this word of caution appears over-simplified, but the author recalls an incident that occurred in a foreign country where three peace officers were transporting, by vehicle, a youth whose appearance was totally deceiving.

It is the practice among certain plainclothesmen in foreign police organizations to carry their weapons in a brief case. The author has never been able to comprehend the reasoning behind this. At any rate, during the course of their travels, apparently all three became so immersed in other events that the youth, even though handcuffed, was able to gain control of a peace officer's weapon. If memory serves right, all three were not only murdered, but their bodies burned as well.

The author does not subscribe to a cardinal rule insofar as travel by sedan, however, certain elements are sufficiently important that they bear consideration. As has previously been stated, the suspect in the majority of instances should be handcuffed with his hands behind his back. If there is only one suspect, it is preferred that he ride in the rear of the sedan with the senior member seated to his right, as is illustrated in the figure titled: "Positions of Suspect and Peace Officer when Traveling by Sedan."

RECOMMENDED
Fig. 39. Restraint: Position of Suspect and Peace Officer when
Traveling by Sedan

It is recognized that this places the suspect directly behind the driver, however, primary consideration is given to the fact that most peace officers carry their weapons on their right side and this seating arrangement offers less accessibility to the suspect.

Where there is more than one suspect they should be seated in the rear with the senior member of the police team seated up front.

This seating arrangement is not recommended in the first instance because it is believed that there is too much of a tendency, while seated up front, to fail to continually observe the rear occupants of the car. In most instances where the driver applies the brake or makes any sharp steering movement, there is an unconscious reaction among all drivers, who are riding as passengers, to look for the cause of the movement.

Where the peace officer is operating independently he has little choice as to the seating arrangement. A word of caution is advised, however, in that, when the suspect is seated to his right, the peace officer should remove his weapon from his holster and place it in a position out-of-reach of the suspect.

Consideration is forthcoming concerning the preparation of a vehicle to be used for transportation of a suspect. Prior to the suspect's entry, the glove compartment should be locked and the vehicle itself should be carefully scrutinized to assure total absence of any object that could be used by the suspect as a weapon. Frequently patrol cars have special mountings for larger weapons that provide a distinct convenience to the suspect.

The author does recommend adoption of the cardinal rule that *a suspect should never be handcuffed to any part of a vehicle that can move.* This applies to automobiles, trains, airplanes, etc. If this rule is not adhered to and the one in a thousand freak accident does take place, the suspect is unnecessarily exposed to extreme danger. Naturally, if this occurs, the peace officer is subject to a serious countercharge.

In arriving at the police station the same air of alertness must exist. Again, there is a tendency to relax believing that no mishap will occur within the protected atmosphere of a police headquarters. However, incidents have been known whereby the peace officer, concentrating on completing the necessary administration required in the arrest, stands in a position immediately adjacent to the prisoner, and bends over, literally placing a weapon in the hands of the suspect.

The tragedy of deaths under these circumstances is particularly emphasized by the fact that, not only does the careless peace officer get killed, but many of his innocent companions are subjected to extremely dangerous risks as a result of his negligence.

Never forget that there is no cure for a fatal mistake. Prior preventative measures are the only means of alleviation. The author has investigated too many murders where the forthcoming excuse started out with: "Well, I took what I thought were reasonable precautions. I never dreamed that any guy in his right mind——."

Unfortunately it turned out that the suspect was not in his right mind, or was so "hopped up" through the use of marijuana (or a narcotic), or felt that he was definitely destined for capital punishment and accordingly believed that he had nothing to lose, or was just simply so panic-stricken that he could no longer think logically, that the slayings were without motive, rhyme or reason.

THE COMPLETE SEARCH

Whenever the suspect is considered armed or particularly dangerous, or in any instance where narcotics or marijuana is suspected, a second search should be made at police headquarters.

This should be accomplished in a room especially prepared by: the absence of any objects that could be used as a weapon, the facility of providing complete privacy, and the absence of any convenience that could be used as a means of the suspect hiding a cache. No weapon should be allowed in the room, instead the peace officers normally "turn in" their weapons at the desk prior to entering the room.

As the search is executed in an effort to satisfy two requirements, the securance of evidence as well as the unequivocal determination that the suspect has no hidden weapons, for future testimony in court it is advised that one peace officer record in notes all evidence found on the suspect.

In this type of search the suspect is required to remove all articles of clothing. These are passed to one peace officer, who carefully reexamines all seams, cuffs, heels, and bulky parts of clothing. In addition, he examines inch by inch every part of the clothing by the "crushing" method.

The other peace officer carefully examines the person of the suspect, starting by running a comb through the suspect's hair and carefully scrutinizing every inch of the suspects' body. He should be alert for bandages, especially flesh colored adhesive tape that could conceal narcotics.

All openings of the body should be carefully scrutinized for the concealment of hidden pouches containing narcotics or even weapons. Where the suspect has a dental bridge or false teeth, he should be required to remove this from his mouth for careful scrutiny by the peace officer.

A systematic search should be made by starting from the top and proceding to the soles, covering each area as cited in the illustration titled: "Points to be Scrutinized in the Complete Search."

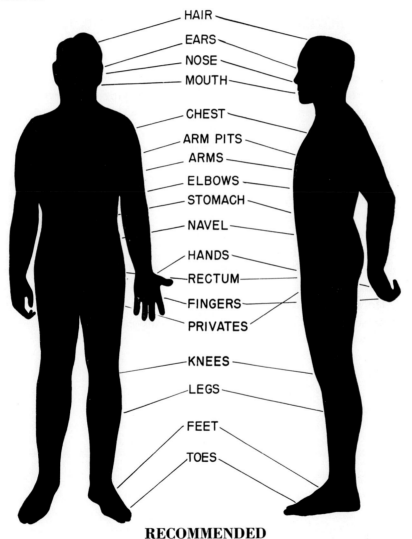

RECOMMENDED

Fig. 40. Search: Points to be Scrutinized in the Complete Search

At the completion of the search the suspect should be provided with prison garb and his own clothing secured until his release.

EXAMINATION

1. Why, at the start of the complete search, should a comb be run through the suspect's hair?
2. When traveling by airplane, should the suspect be handcuffed to the seat or the arm rest?
3. Where there are one suspect and two peace officers traveling by sedan, where should the suspect be seated? Why?
4. Where there is a lone peace officer conveying a suspect, what special factors should be considered concerning the weapon?
5. In the "search room" for the complete search, what special precautions should be provided for the security of the peace officers' weapons?
6. Why does the author advocate that the senior member be seated in the rear of a sedan unless it is absolutely necessary that he be seated otherwise?
7. Give three causes that could result in the suspect committing totally illogical acts.
8. Why is the use of a notebook advocated during a complete search?
9. Does the author advocate the use of a female chaperone to be present while a female suspect is subjected to a complete search?

CHAPTER 8

SPECIAL PRECAUTIONS AND PROCEDURES

THE FEMALE SUSPECT

Where possible, the female suspect should be arrested by female personnel. It is recognized, however, that frequently this cannot be accomplished. Where it is necessary for the male peace officer to execute an arrest of this sort, he should avoid, as much as possible, unnecessary physical contact; however, modesty becomes too expensive a luxury if it threatens the lives of the peace officer and the suspect.

The wall search is very rarely if ever accomplished, however, the peace officer is perfectly justified in examining the handbag or coat (after being removed from the person of the female suspect) in an effort to determine if any weapons are hidden therein.

Determination as to the use of handcuffs should again remain totally at the discretion of the arresting peace officer. The author is aware that usually the female does not have the strength to accomplish an attack as would be forthcoming with a male suspect; however, she can be just as quick, if not faster, in grabbing the peace officer's weapon or "yanking" the steering wheel of a moving vehicle.

THE DANGER OF OVER-EAGERNESS

There is a tendency among some automobile drivers to oversteer. The consequences are not particularly severe, except that they unnecessarily tire the driver. There is a tendency among some peace officers to become over-eager during the arrest and the consequences here can and frequently do become extremely serious.

The author is not so much concerned here with brutality to the suspect as it is believed that this falls entirely within the purview of responsible supervisors; but he is rather concerned with the fact that the suspect versed in judo is prone to take advantage of these unnecessary movements, and they can cause an otherwise safe arrest to abruptly change into a dangerous and even fatal one.

A very common error made is, as shown in the figure titled: "Wrong Position Because of Extended Weapon," where the ar-

NOT RECOMMENDED

Fig. 41.   Precautions: Wrong Position Because of Extended Weapon

resting peace officer extends the weapon away from his body and close to the person of the suspect, it invites the judo expert to execute a fairly easy judo movement as is presented in the figure titled: "Loss of Weapon Made Possible by Entending Same."

The competent peace officer always uses his free hand to pro-

NOT RECOMMENDED

Fig. 42. Precautions: Loss of Weapon Made Possible by Extending Same

tect his weapon, especially in the event that he is "rushed." This affords him ample opportunity to fire the weapon, particularly, as previously cited, if he keeps the weapon close to his side.

Whether the arrest is serious or minor, standing squarely and directly in front of the suspect, as is shown in the figure titled:

NOT RECOMMENDED

Fig. 43.   Precautions: Direct Stance; Too Close to Suspect

"Direct Stance; Too Close to Suspect," invites an attack that is
executed simply by the suspect leaping forward and pressing
against the chests of the peace officers, as shown in the figure

NOT RECOMMENDED

Fig. 44. Precautions: Result of the Incorrect Approach

titled: "Result of the Incorrect Approach." Although execution of this movement appears improbable, very little practice can accomplish successful results.

RECOMMENDED

Fig. 45. Precautions: Close Approach to the Suspect; Angular Stance

The correct procedure, as is shown in the figure titled: "Close Approach to the Suspect; Angular Stance," has the peace officers spread and, whether operating as a team or independently, the peace officer faces the suspect in a position resembling a boxer's stance, which is slightly angular with one foot drawn back a minor distance behind the other.

NOT RECOMMENDED

Fig. 46. Precautions: Steering Suspect by the Arms

"Steering," as shown in the figure titled: "Steering Suspect by the Arms," is not only commonly shown in television dramas, but unexcusably is as frequently shown in newsreels depicting actual events.

NOT RECOMMENDED

Fig. 47. Precautions: Collision Resulting from Steering

The break is exceedingly simple; the suspect simply by squeezing his arms, clamps the peace officers' hands to his sides and takes a sharp step backwards. The result, as illustrated in the figure titled: "Collision Resulting from Steering," can be extremely embarassing and even disastrous.

NOT RECOMMENDED

Fig. 48.   Precautions: Pushing by Hand on Chest

The hand placed on the suspect's chest while pushing, as illustrated in the figure titled: "Pushing by Hand on Chest," is a distinct invitation for a broken wrist.

NOT RECOMMENDED

Fig. 49. Precautions: Wrist Breaking Hold Made Possible by Placing
Hand on Chest

In order to satisfy this request, the suspect simply places both
of his hands over and freezes the peace officer's hand against his
chest, concluding the movement by a sharp drop downwards, as
illustrated in the figure titled: "Wrist Breaking Hold Made Possible by Placing Hand on Chest."

NOT RECOMMENDED
Fig. 50. Precautions: Guiding by Hand on Shoulder

The common practice of laying a hand on the suspect's shoulder, as is shown in the figure titled: "Guiding by Hand on Shoulder," is as equal an invitation, the satisfaction of which can be easily accomplished by the suspect freezing the peace officer's hand on his shoulder and bringing his other arm around in a sharp

NOT RECOMMENDED

Fig. 51. Precautions: Arm Breaking Hold made Possible by Hand
on Shoulder

circular downward "chop," as is shown in the figure titled: "Arm Breaking Hold made Possible by Hand on Shoulder."

In conclusion, no better advice is forthcoming than to repeat the words that appear at the very beginning of the book. The peace officer, in attempting to survive the arrest, must constantly be aware that the biggest killers are CARELESSNESS, OVER-CONFIDENCE, and LACK OF TRAINING.

Good luck!

EXAMINATION

1. If a male peace officer arrests a female suspected of being armed, what two articles are definitely searched?
2. Is the peace officer ever justified in handcuffing a female suspect?
3. If on his own the peace officer decides that he is justified in handcuffing a female suspect, what special procedures should he adopt?
4. What is the proper stance required when the peace officer approaches close to the suspect?
5. Describe the positions of the hands and their intended use where the peace officer carries weapon in hand.

APPENDIX

CARDINAL RULES

1. Only by constant training and retraining can the devastating effects of tension be overcome to the extent that the peace officer is able to safely and effectively accomplish a dangerous arrest.
2. The peace officer must never forget that, in executing the arrest, he is accomplishing a professional job and not reduce the transaction to a conflict of personalities.
3. The peace officer's attitude in approaching the arrest should encompass firmness, mature judgment, tact, and self-control.
4. The most dangerous suspect is a severely frightened or panic-stricken one.
5. An arrest is an act that deprives an individual of his liberty.
6. Once a suspect is arrested, no favors or special requests are to be granted.
7. During an arrest a threat is never made unless the peace officer intends and has the means of fulfilling it.
8. During an arrest the tone of the peace officer's voice should not imply that a request is being made; instead, it should indicate that a command has been given with confidence that it will be carried out.
9. During the arrest the peace officer raises his voice only to make himself heard, never because emotion has overwhelmed him.
10. A quiet tone of voice has an over-all calming effect.
11. The arresting peace officer imparts a professional air by neat appearance, definite movements, and an air of alertness.
12. Unless the arrest is accomplished during daylight by a uniformed peace officer, every arrest is initiated by the peace officer identifying himself.
13. Normally, as an element of every arrest, the suspect is explained under what charge he is being arrested.

14. An arrest is completed either by the suspect overtly indicating his acceptance of this status, or by the peace officer "touching" him.

15. As a matter of competent police procedure, all civilian peace officers cite the suspect's rights under the Fifth Amendment to the Constitution of the United States, while all military mandatorily cite their rights under the Thirty-first Article.

16. A serious arrest is an arrest for a felony; a minor arrest is an arrest for any offense less than a felony.

17. No type of arrest is ever sufficiently minor as to allow the peace officer, for even a moment, to lower his guard or not be constantly alert for danger.

18. The recommended procedure to be applied where force is required is: first, to explain to the suspect what is desired of him; if not complied with, to repeat the command together with a warning that force will be applied; if still not obeyed, to effect the actual force.

19. Force should never be resorted to except to overcome resistance.

20. Force should never be resorted to except as a last resort, and then only the minimum applied.

21. When actual physical resistance ceases, the peace officer immediately ceases to apply physical force.

22. In a minor arrest, the force that can be applied to overcome resistance must be short of that force which could result in death.

23. "Warning shots" should not be resorted to; instead, the peace officer should utilize verbal warnings.

24. A peace officer is never justified in jeopardizing the life of an innocent party solely as a means of effecting an arrest.

25. Unless the suspect is known to be armed and dangerous, in the minor arrest the peace officer approaches the scene of the arrest with his weapon remaining in its holster.

26. In the serious arrest the weapon is taken from the holster prior to the approach to the scene of the arrest and remains in the hand of the arresting peace officer throughout the arrest.

27. When capturing a dangerous suspect it is absolutely essential

to immediately acquire control as soon as the range of the voice and the weapon make this feasible.

28. The calculated risk is only justified where no other avenue is available.

29. In approaching the serious arrest with an automatic pistol, the safety catch is "on," the hammer "cocked" to the rear, and a bullet rests in the chamber.

30. In approaching the serious arrest when armed with a revolver, the hammer is "forward" so that, if fired, it is accomplished by firing "double action."

31. In approaching the serious arrest the trigger finger rests on the trigger.

32. Caution should be exercised to prevent obstructions from interfering with the movements of the hammer of a revolver.

33. In teamwork there should be previously designated a senior and junior member.

34. The senior member should direct the actions, delegating appropriate responsibilitits to the junior member.

35. The junior member should cover all other suspects not being dealt with by the senior member.

36. Movements are accomplished by the junior member automatically taking his cue from the senior member.

37. In teamwork every effort should be exercised to maintain a "spread."

38. Where a weapon is displayed and it becomes necessary for one member of the team, whether senior or junior, to cross the line of fire of the other member, the member in the rear always points his weapon up out of range until the other member moves out of the line of fire.

39. The weapon always is held close to the body (and never used as a pointer) with the free hand acting as a cover.

40. Upon entering a room where a serious arrest is to be accomplished, action is always started by the senior member covering all occupants of the room, immobilizing them, while the junior member immediately searches all possible areas that could hide an accomplice.

41. All arrests should be immediately followed by a preliminary search.

42. The only type of search that provides the necessary advantage of keeping the suspect "off-balance" and the peace officer "on-balance" throughout the search is the wall search.

43. The proper wall search stance requires the suspect's palms flat against the wall, hands spread to the extreme, the head down, the back and rump unarched, the feet spread to the extreme and extended back away from the wall to the point that the use of the suspect's hands is required to keep from falling.

44. In executing the wall search, an imaginary dividing line is drawn down the middle of the suspect's body and the peace officer never crosses this line throughout the search.

45. Where more than one suspect is to be searched, only one suspect is allowed to move at a time.

46. Where more than one suspect is to be searched, all suspects should be required to keep their heads down and be prohibited from exchanging conversation.

47. Every inch of clothing should be grasped in the hand and actually crushed.

48. The cuff, sleeve, belt, shoe and sock are properly searched by insertion of the fingers or hand and "crushed."

49. During the search for a serious arrest, the hand nearest the wall is used to make the search. The hand farthest from the wall is used to hold the weapon. The foot nearest the wall is used to engage the suspect's foot.

50. When searching lower extremities, the peace officer maintains his balance by assuming a crouch instead of bending or stooping over.

51. The use of restraining devices should be left to the discretion of the arresting peace officer.

52. Handcuffs should be applied with the "jaw" open and never "snapped" on.

53. Handcuffs should never be fastened so tightly as to obstruct the normal flow of blood, nor so loosely as to allow them being "slipped" over the hands.

54. When one handcuff is applied, the other is to be held firmly by the peace officer.

55. The suspect's hands are always handcuffed behind him.

56. Whenever handcuffs are applied, they are to be "double locked."

57. Whenever a substitute restraining device is resorted to, it should be applied by the use of separate loops for each wrist.

58. In a serious arrest the weapon is returned to the holster prior to the application of the handcuffs.

59. A vehicle is prepared for transporting a suspect by securing all objects and weapons that could be accessible to the suspect and locking the glove compartment.

60. When a lone peace officer transports suspects in a vehicle, the weapon should be removed from the holster and secured by being placed in a position inaccessible to the suspects.

61. A suspect should never be handcuffed to any part of a vehicle that can move.

62. Where a suspect is arrested on a charge involving the use of narcotics, marijuana, or is known to have been armed or dangerous, he should be subjected to a second search called the "complete" search.

63. No weapons should be brought into the room where a complete search is to be made.

64. A notebook record should be made of all evidence gained during any search.

65. The peace officer should avoid unnecessary physical contact with the suspect, whether the suspect is male or female, as to do so invites a counter-attack.

66. The three big killers in police work are carelessness, overconfidence, and lack of training.

EXAMINATION ANSWERS

Chapter 1

1. Accomplishing the arrest.

2. Training and alertness.

3. No. Quite frequently the experienced peace officer becomes

over-confident while the rookie has a better awareness of the prevalent dangers.

4. There are no signs. Any arrest, no matter how simple and innocent appearing during the initial stages can, without warning, become dangerous.

5. There are none. Even the most innocent appearance can be the mask of a true psychopath.

6. None. He usually dies.

Chapter 2

1. At the very beginning.

2. He has through experience gained the over-all belief that he will be obeyed, whereas the rookie has doubts which are sometimes reflected in his actions.

3. The danger of pitting one's self against the suspect emotionally instead of the correct procedure whereby the arresting officer approaches the arrest with an attitude of, "This is a job I have to do and not a personal fight between the suspect and me."

4. None, until the suspect is brought to the police station.

5. A threat is never made unless the peace officer has the means of carrying it out and intends to carry it out.

6. A panic-stricken one.

7. The tone of voice should imply that a command is being given, not that the suspect is being asked in a question-like manner to comply.

8. It implies self-confidence and has an over-all calming effect.

9. Muscular tone should be relaxed. The subject should be faced squarely, hands resting at the sides. The club should remain sheathed. Movements should be unhurried. There should be a general air of alertness, and yet there should remain a comfortable stance.

Chapter 3

1. His identification as having the authoritative status to make the arrest, especially by plainclothesmen and uniformed personnel at night.

2. The author regards this procedure adversely, believing that it can illegally jeopardize the lives of innocent bystanders.

3. An arrest for a felony.
4. An arrest for a misdemeanor or other lesser offenses.
5. There is no difference.
6. Only after all other means have proved unsuccessful and it is necessary to overcome resistance.
7. In a serious arrest.
8. None.
9. When the resistance ceases.
10. The peace officer is never justified in endangering the lives of innocent bystanders.
11. There is no modification.

Chapter 4

1. Prior to arrival at the scene.
2. Only within the range of his voice and his weapon.
3. There is no possible way to *see* where a weapon may be hidden. The peace officer must be prepared to take the necessary steps to prevent a hidden weapon from being used.
4. The suspect's hands. All dangerous movement must evolve from them.
5. Only those that he cannot possibly avoid. He is never justified in taking an unnecessary chance.
6. Well in advance to arrival at the scene of arrest, as the noise of placing a bullet in the chamber can give away the element of surprise.
7. The hammer is to rest forward and, if necessary, the weapon is to be fired "double action."
8. In both instances the trigger finger rests on the trigger.
9. Except in one rare instance (during the wall search) he carries the automatic in his right hand, as the safety catch is more accessible.
10. Careful observation should be forthcoming to preclude an obstruction from interfering with movement of the hammer.
11. One member should be designated as the leader or senior member, and the other is designated as the junior member.
12. The member in the rear always points his weapon "up" out of range until the member in front has passed out of the line of fire.

13. On all other suspects with whom the senior member is not actively concerned.

14. The senior member covers and freezes all visible occupants of the room while the junior member searches for and flushes out any hidden accomplices.

15. They always try to spread out taking positions in adjacent corners.

16. The weapon is never used as a pointer but remains covering the suspect while the other hand is used to designate directions.

17. The same as in a serious arrest.

Chapter 5

1. There are no signs. Frequently the expert can physically appear to be a rather fragile, small-statured individual, male or female.

2. Only his previous training and alertness during the arrest and search. Failure to provide this can result in his easily being disarmed.

3. The wall search.

4. Even a wall is not required. Any object that can support the weight of the suspect is satisfactory.

5. (1) It keeps the suspect "off-balance" throughout the search.
   (2) It keeps the peace officer "on-balance" throughout the search.
   (3) It affords a means of immobilizing the suspect's hands and feet throughout the search.
   (4) It affords a means of keeping the suspect from observing the movements of the peace officer.
   (5) It affords a means of "throwing" the suspect at any time.
   (6) It provides the best means of immobilizing other suspects waiting to be searched.
   (7) It provides the best preparatory position for the next step —handcuffing.
   (8) It provides the greatest handicaps to the suspect contemplating a counter-attack.
   (9) It provides the easiest accessibility to all areas of the suspect's person for search.

    (10) It requires the suspect's entire musculature to support him throughout the search.

6. He remains in an "on-balance" position and is afforded the added means of the muscles in his arms and waist in attacking the peace officer.

7. They should be spread apart as far as possible and back to the greatest extent away from the wall.

8. Directions should not be contingent upon pointing as this affords the suspect the means of turning and observing the peace officer's position.

9. Immediately upon completion of the arrest.

10. (a) In the hand of the searching peace officer.
    (b) In the holster of the searching peace officer.
    (c) In the hand of the searching peace officer.

11. Only one suspect is to be moved at a time. Before a suspect is to be moved both peace officers step back away from the line.

12. He draws an imaginary line down the middle of the body and does not cross this line throughout the search. In addition, when searching the lower extremities, he assumes a crouching position.

13. (1) He can call upon the aid of a passerby to communicate his needs to headquarters.
    (2) Where available, he can make use of his radio transmitter to seek aid from his headquarters.
    (3) He can disregard the search and, while being especially alert, transport the prisoners to headquarters.

14. The hand nearest the wall and the foot nearest the wall.

15. The senior member searches the right side while standing on the right side of the suspect, with the junior member taking up his position on the left side of the suspect. While searching the left side of the suspect, the senior member takes up a position on the left side of the suspect, and the junior member moves to the right side of the suspect.

16. The suspect's hat.

17. His hand and the area between his fingers.

18. The sole of his shoe.

19. When searching the right side of the suspect.

20. When there is more than one suspect the junior member, in order to avoid bringing the senior member into his line of fire, takes up his position at the end of the line of suspects (waiting to be searched) nearest the senior member.

21. By the peace officer pressing his ankle bone tight against the suspect's ankle bone, he can "feel" any of the suspect's major movements.

22. None. All areas of the clothing should be searched by "crushing" the clothing.

23. The finger is inserted inside of the shoe and moved around the entire inside of the shoe.

24. The hand is to be inserted and every inch is to be "crushed."

25. Absolutely.

26. The searcher steps back and instructs the suspect to lift his foot.

27. It provides a "short cut."

28. The prone search.

29. He states that this procedure is a disadvantage as, with the arms extended above the head, the suspect's movement is more quickly discernible.

Chapter 6

1. Practically none at all.

2. He describes that the unnecessary "parading" of a suspect to public view is humiliating whether the suspect is handcuffed or not.

3. The author subscribes to the doctrine that the use of handcuffs should be left entirely to the discretion of the arresting peace officer, as he is the only one in a position to logically evaluate the intent of the suspect.

4. The handcuff should never be "snapped" on. Instead, the "jaw" should be opened prior to application.

5. It should be tight enough to prevent slipping over the hand, yet loose enough to allow free blood flow.

6. It provides the suspect with a valuable weapon with which he is quite capable of cracking the peace officer's skull.

7. It facilitates his movement (through doors and in and out of

automobiles) and also provides a valuable weapon to be used against the peace officer.

8. It provides the suspect with a means of using one foot as a fulcrum and "slinging" the peace officer.
9. The suspect's hands should always be handcuffed behind him.
10. They should always be "double locked."
11. The prong is used to "double lock" the handcuffs by inserting it in a small hole found in the stem of the bracelets.
12. The key is first turned counter-clockwise until a distinct "click" is felt, and then it is turned clockwise to open it.
13. If the "jaw" moves freely in one direction, the handcuff is "single locked."
14. It is much easier to "pick" handcuffs that are "single locked" than those that are "double locked."
15. There should be a separate loop for each wrist.
16. The "wall" position.
17. In the holster.
18. (1) "Take your right hand off the wall and place it in the small of your back."
    (2) "Move up and put your head against the wall."
    (3) "Take your left hand off of the wall and place it in the small of your back.
    (4) "Stand up and face the wall."
19. The same as question 18 above.
20. Immediately after he is searched.

Chapter 7

1. This is the only sure method of discovering small objects hidden in the hair.
2. A cardinal rule is that the suspect should never be handcuffed to any part of any vehicle that can move.
3. He should be seated behind the driver so that he cannot easily gain accessibility to the weapon of the peace officer seated to his right.
4. He should take such steps as to remove the weapon from his holster, if the suspect is seated to his right, and properly secure the weapon.

5. Weapons should not be brought into the room but, instead, should be "checked in" at the police desk.
6. Because there is a tendency for all passengers to observe the driver's movements.
7. (1) Because the suspect believes that he is definitely destined for capital punishment and has nothing to lose.
   (2) Because the suspect is emotionally disturbed.
   (3) Because the suspect is under the influence of a drug or alcohol.
   (4) Because the suspect is hysterically panic-stricken.
8. So as to properly record, in accordance with the "rules of evidence," all evidence discovered as a result of the complete search.
9. The author does not recommend this procedure; instead, all female suspects, when subjected to the complete search, should be searched only by female personnel.

Chapter 8

1. Handbag and overcoat (after being removed from her person).
2. Yes, under any circumstances where he suspects her intentions to seriously jeopardize her own or his welfare.
3. None. The same procedure utilized with male suspects is applicable under these circumstances.
4. The peace officer should stand at a slight angle in relation to the suspect, with his feet in a "boxer's" stance.
5. The hand holding the weapon remains close to the side of the peace officer; the other hand guards the weapon and is used to ward off sudden attacks—providing sufficient time to fire the weapon with the other hand.

INDEX